MAKING PARTNERSHIPS
WITH SERVICE USERS
AND ADVOCACY GROUPS WORK

of related interest

A Practical Guide to Delivering Personalisation
Person-Centred Practice in Health and Social Care
Helen Sanderson and Jaimee Lewis
ISBN 978 1 84905 194 1
eISBN 978 0 85700 422 2

Mental Health, Service User Involvement and Recovery
Edited by Jenny Weinstein
ISBN 978 1 84310 688 3
eISBN 978 0 85700 212 9

Hearing the Person with Dementia
Person-Centred Approaches to Communication for Families and Caregivers
Bernie McCarthy
ISBN 978 1 84905 186 6
eISBN 978 0 85700 499 4

Person Centred Planning and Care Management with People with Learning Disabilities
Edited by Paul Cambridge and Steven Carnaby
ISBN 978 1 84310 131 4
eISBN 978 1 84642 140 2

Person-Centred Dementia Care
Making Services Better
Dawn Brooker
ISBN 978 1 84310 337 0
eISBN 978 1 84642 588 2
Bradford Dementia Group Good Practice Guides series

Enriched Care Planning for People with Dementia
A Good Practice Guide to Delivering Person-Centred Care
Hazel May, Paul Edwards and Dawn Brooker
ISBN 978 1 84310 405 6
eISBN 978 1 84642 960 6
Bradford Dementia Group Good Practice Guides series

Co-Production and Personalisation in Social Care
Changing Relationships in the Provision of Social Care
Edited by Susan Hunter and Pete Ritchie
ISBN 978 1 84310 558 9
eISBN 978 1 84642 721 3

MAKING PARTNERSHIPS
WITH SERVICE USERS
AND ADVOCACY GROUPS WORK

*How to Grow Genuine and Respectful
Relationships in Health and Social Care*

Julie Gosling and Jackie Martin

Jessica Kingsley *Publishers*
London and Philadelphia

First published in 2012
by Jessica Kingsley Publishers
116 Pentonville Road
London N1 9JB, UK
and
400 Market Street, Suite 400
Philadelphia, PA 19106, USA

www.jkp.com

Copyright © Julie Gosling and Jackie Martin 2012

Library of Congress Cataloging in Publication Data
Gosling, Julie, 1950-
Making partnerships with service users and advocacy groups work : how to grow genuine and respectful relationships in health and social care / Julie Gosling and Jackie Martin.
p. cm.
Includes index.
ISBN 978-1-84905-193-4 (alk. paper)
1. Social service--Great Britain--Planning--Citizen participation. 2. Health planning--Great Britain--Citizen participation. 3. Social advocacy--Great Britain. 4. Public-private sector collaboration--Great Britain. I. Martin, Jackie, 1959- II. Title.
HV245.G664 2012
361.941068--dc23
2011042567

British Library Cataloguing in Publication Data
A CIP catalogue record for this book is available from the British Library

ISBN 978 1 84905 193 4
eISBN 978 0 85700 608 0

Printed and bound in Great Britain

CONTENTS

ACKNOWLEDGEMENTS

JULIE

I deeply and humbly give thanks to Gina Hardesty, Mark Lymbery, Jackie Martin, Dave Milburn, Ian Nesbitt, Michael Preston Shoot, Reshma Patel, June Sadd and Jenny Weinstein, true allies over the years who have understood and demonstrated in a variety of ways an active commitment to the practice and principles of enabling partnerships within professional publications and media productions. And I am more than forever grateful to so many dear colleagues and partners of Advocacy In Action, past and present, and additionally members of The Long Distance Gang and the Older People's Partnership Services (OPPS) – without all of these loyal friends and collaborators, my own personal contribution amounts to very little.

I dedicate my work to 'Corncrake Sean' – a free and noble spirit.

JACKIE

I wish to acknowledge the unswerving support of my family and friends. I dedicate this book to them with love.

With special thanks to Fade and the Hard to Find Cafe in Nottingham where we found inspiration, good coffee, a warm welcome and spent many hours writing this book together!

INTRODUCTION

PARTNERSHIPS AND GROWING SPACES

As the book unfolds you will come to know some very different partnerships. Their stories are interwoven throughout, describing celebration, frustration, trust, hope, anger, joy, feelings of connectedness or separation, of belonging but also of not belonging. The partners tell their stories to let others learn from their experience. The partnerships themselves tell you what has worked well and not so well and what makes a good partnership, but also what points to poor partnership.

This collection of narratives seeks to explore the nature of partnership and to define the conditions that enable people to come together in honest, fair and creative allegiances. It is important that you familiarise yourself with all the partnerships discussed in this book (see p.17 for more details on the individual partnerships) before going on to read the rest of the text.

Julie

It is true that these days the word 'partnership' is used at every opportunity. We use it, I suppose, to try and make positive steps towards other people. I guess it's an attempt to try and redress power imbalances. But I am beginning to realise that increasingly it's becoming a way of getting people to comply and cooperate. I am beginning to feel very worried about words such as 'partnership' and 'involvement'. What do they truly mean? What sort of arrangements between human beings do they describe? I want to be careful about where and when I use the word partnership in future.

Some years ago, I received a telephone call from a local authority training officer. She informed me that as part of her department's commitment to partnership she was able to offer me a free place on a course entitled 'Person-Centred Planning and Service User Empowerment'. I thanked her good-humouredly and said I was one of the people who had been active in the early 1990s in pioneering the new concepts of person-centred values and practice, and had since taught them at undergraduate, post-graduate and post-qualifying (PQ) levels in universities across the UK and Europe! There was a few moments silence, and then she responded, 'Yes, but we want to empower you! Surely you'd like to take advantage of our knowledge and skills – that's what involvement's about, isn't it?' I politely refused her invitation and I thought back to our radical ideas of the 1990s and wondered what had become of them.

So are we talking about real allegiance or are 'partnership' and 'involvement' just things that some people 'do' to others? By the end of this book I hope you will agree we have celebrated some truly great partnership practice. But just to start, let's think about some of the reasons put forward for *not* involving people in things that affect their lives and well-being. There are many to choose from!

Involvement *as exploitation* intimates that some get used by others, and it is true that at its worst, involvement and partnership *can* be highly exploitative. But involvement at its best enables a reclaiming of control. People become confident and active citizens, knowledgeable, skilled and innovative. The opportunity just to 'give' to and with others is very important in itself for people who usually find themselves on the 'receiving' end of assistance.

Involvement *as tokenism* implies that partnership is just something peripheral to the 'real work' done by the 'important people'. Good involvement conversely not only *becomes* the real work, it makes *all* work more productive and satisfying. The tokenism excuse also suggests that some people are 'less able' than others to become involved. But where tokenism is used to devalue the involvement of less well easily heard people, it becomes downright oppressive. People can have place and purpose in partnerships without uttering a single word. Some find technical competence and go on to find a voice. Others interact physically but enable a consideration of the reactions they evoke. Others still embody the silent right to witness and be witnessed, while some offer support to their partners with a hug, a yell, or the world's best smile.

Understanding has many layers. Where abstract ideas and concepts may fly over people's heads, human feelings can be shared, empathised and nurtured. Partnership at its best emphasises our common humanity.

Involvement has many levels, not just the visible spoken interactions – and to hoist involvement on the spear of tokenism shows a calculated decision *not* to include others. But I personally have never met anyone who could not be involved, as many of the partners in this book celebrate.

Involvement *as voyeurism* hints at the manner in which we avidly consume the lives of others. Where people expose intimate personal stories, listeners can feel uncomfortable, and feel themselves laid bare. But it is as natural to feel moved and upset by the appalling things human beings do to one another as it is to be inspired by the resilience, strength and spirit of survival. Storytellers hope their lives will help people learn how to treat one another better, help to protect the most vulnerable in society and move to insist that those in power confront the terrible betrayals and neglect of the past and present. Without a doubt, some stories are painful to hear – but they promote mutual healing and reconciliation.

When we survivors get asked if we need professional therapists to attend to the wounds and the thorns of our pasts, this is often a subtle way of blame shifting. By claiming and redefining the story within professional territory, the storyteller is rendered 'vulnerable' and impotent, and stories become the 'problems' that only experts can untangle, rather than the powerful testimonies of injustice and inhumanity which have inspired bottom-up solutions. We all have a responsibility to hear the truth and to do something about it. Far from inviting voyeurism, partnership is a mutual way of engaging one another in open honest engagements that demand real personal responses, described by one partner as 'face-to-face, nowhere to hide connection'.

Involvement *as living in the past* encourages people to forgive and forget. 'Leave the past behind!' we are told. 'It's too upsetting!' But upsetting for whom? Reclaiming and validating the past and making sense of it in our own way is the platform on which we build our todays and tomorrows. The past celebrates survival and it is our individual and collective histories that represent the politics of our anger, our pride and our power. 'Haven't you got any happy positive stories?' we are asked. But there are, for the finding, moments of inspiration, strength and compassion in even the darkest tales. It's just that listeners get hooked on the guilt at times. We think powerful partners want to be liked and want the rest of us to be happy, because it helps them to feel they are doing a good job. But at times it can be awful being told to 'cheer up' or that it's 'not that bad!' when in reality life *is* that bad. Is it that 'happy and content' equates with 'grateful and compliant'? We tell our partners that we don't require them to make us happy – we just want the same opportunities as other people and we reserve the right to be fed up when we need to be!

Involvement as *pushing the politics* intimates that partnership should be absolutely values free! A voluntary organisation manager once told me that involvement is 'saying things about yourself, without making other people angry'! But this means that power stays where it has always been. Our past experience has shown us that partnership is fine when you are deciding on the colour of the door, but less welcome when it defines who should hold the keys. Sharing power means 'letting go' and losing power, and that without a doubt makes some individuals feel angry and terrified. Of course involvement in the things that shape our lives is political – it is not about concession or permission; it is all about change and the absolutely fundamental right to inclusion in matters that affect us. And decades before legislation imposed partnership, we, the people at the bottom, were insisting on, showing the way to, and promoting it.

Involvement *as retribution* suggests we're in it for the 'payback'! The underlying fear seems to be, 'After all we do for you and no matter how hard we try, you just come along and clobber us!' Now where strong partners are themselves beginning to feel demoralised and powerless, then the involvement of others *is* capable of creating negative emotional response, fuelled by frustration of being held to account for failure. But partnership at its best unites the shared experiences of all partners as 'survivors' and builds up the allegiances that promote mutual empowerment. Avoiding involvement to avoid negativity only allows powerful people to build up unrealistic views of themselves and the value of their contribution to the lives of others.

Involvement as *over emotional* and *under intellectual* indicates how little value is attached by some to their own feelings and the feelings of others. There are many levels of involvement at both head and heart levels, and professional education sometimes neglects this. One worker reflects:

> My 'intellectual' training has detached and disconnected me from my own experience and yours. But I can now feel myself rattling the academic chains that have prohibited me from opening up and working with you on a humane and empathic level.

We tell our partners that connecting to their own fragility is the experiential bridge from which they will reach out and connect with us.

Involvement is 'unnecessary because we know how you feel'! Do you? Who exactly is it who 'knows' how we feel? When partners say, for instance, 'We are all the same at the end of the day,' we ask them: Do you know what it feels like to leave this room and go out to sleep on the streets, or return to a bullying restrictive care home, or try and bag a few days' labouring work because at 72 years of age you still haven't claimed your State Pension? Do you honestly know any of this?

We are not inside your policy documents; we are real people living real lives, surviving however we can. Only by listening to us and learning from and with us will you ever truly know how we feel.

Involvement *as unwise*, because 'we are worried about you', suggests our conditions need managing and that there is every chance that things will get out of hand and we will damage ourselves – or others – or do irreparable harm to professional credibility. But does 'worried about you' mean that 'you shouldn't be here'? For those of us used to living in our own skins, our personal conditions are far less a problem than other people's worried responses to them.

Involvement *as blurring the boundaries* reminds us how we all like to feel secure. But partnership can set new and sometimes scary boundaries and this isn't always easy for less powerful partners or for those who wear their professional status like a protective layer. The sudden death of a partner is all the more tragic because more powerful colleagues did not involve themselves as he became ill. 'Work boundaries' restricted them from checking up when he stopped coming into the office. So what does involvement truly mean? 'Part-time partnerships', office hours and activities only? Or reaching to one another over the boundaries and into liberated new spaces?

Involvement is *not for us, after all*. Some partners choose not to get involved, or to *dis*-involve. There are many reasons for this.

We move on. Involvement becomes stressful. Lives improve and fill with new possibilities. We get disillusioned with our partners. Other things take priority. We start to feel used and abused. We simply run out of useful things to say.

Non-involvement and *dis*-involvement do not necessarily indicate lack of motivation or capacity. It can be about disempowerment, distrust or disappointment, or an active response to this, or conversely, occasioned by positives. *Dis*-involvement can be a very powerful and effective choice. There is nothing particularly rewarding, however, about distrust!

But why might some partners distrust others? Well this brings us to the 'Manifesto of Involvement – How Not to Do It!'

The first precept is *incorporation* – 'bringing into', 'subsuming' or 'ingesting'.

I remember how proud we used to feel at the beginning of the 1990s with all those early invitations to sit on forums and attend planning events, and how wearisome and frustrating it became when time after time again, nothing happened as a result.

It was over 20 years ago, in 1990, when I gave a tongue-in-cheek presentation to the Association of Metropolitan Authorities, entitled: 'How to Use Partnership to Avoid Power-Sharing – Useful Pointers for Large Organisations'.

In addition to the usual 'our-plans–your-views', I spoke about the helpful strategies of 'fund-and-control' and 'get a paid worker in there quick!' I then went on to discuss how the very language, ideas and energy of popular movements had been sucked into the organisational machine, but with all the gristly bits spat out and the residue scarfed back out to us in a bland, diluted and narcotic mush. Re-reading my paper recently, I was utterly dismayed to see that it all still applied down to the last full stop.

So how exactly does incorporation work? Well it brings in its little group of 'partners', 'advisers', 'consultants', using the words as brightly coloured sweet wrappers to disguise the harsh taste that, at its heart, is nothing of good substance – that *nothing* has really changed. Language is the invisible shot which tranquillises us into believing we are active partners rather than captive participants.

A practitioner recently shared with us:

> I can see the part I have played in maintaining the status quo. As a professional, I have used language like 'partnership working' and 'promoting choice' to veil the truth that these rarely happen.

The language of incorporation lulls us into believing that we are involved, valued and able to punch far over and above our own weight! But when we realise that involvement and partnership are limited and moreover less than honest, then we start to lose trust. However, incorporation is only the beginning!

The next principle of 'How Not to Do Involvement!' is the even more blatant act of *colonisation* — takeover, misappropriation and theft. And in exactly the same way that our physical, emotional and spiritual struggles have been turned into 'conditions' to be defined and controlled by professionals, so our imaginative responses and endurances have subsequently been stolen from us and claimed as 'expert territory'. The emancipatory solutions of 'self-advocacy', 'peer support', 'recovery', 'personalisation', 'advance directives' and 'person-centred planning' are all rooted firmly within community and service-user knowledge, yet every one has now been 'taken over' in what can only be termed as the ultimate colonisation of our values, our creativity, our empowerments and even our survivals.

A partner of many years' experience reflects:

> How many times have I been thanked for a piece of work when I hadn't done anything, it was the service user who achieved, all I did was just help along the way. Yet I have taken the thanks. But now, rather than feeling proud, I wonder, was I proprietary?

Another partner, considering the same, discovers that: 'it was the service users who jumped through the hoops while we workers won the medals.' But the ultimate betrayal has been the educators and academics and power-mongers, who have made their name and their name alone on the back of ordinary people's ideas, innovations and survival. We *do* know who they are and they *are* now barred for life from our partnerships.

The final tenet in 'How Not to Do Involvement!' is *commodification* — the depersonalising and objectifying mentality that mutates dynamic *processes* of emancipation into commodities or *products* to meet selfish power-retentive interests. Let us consider 'advocacy', for instance — the right to speak out or be represented but now traded out through statutory commissioning in bargain basement deals, or the purse strings mentality of 'individual budgets' that costs out and timetables every precious moment of freedom and personal choice. One professional partner noted recently that: 'despite all the rhetoric, things are not improving for people; if anything, processes are actually becoming more rigid!'

Incorporation, colonisation, commodification — lots of reasons *not* to get involved as partners! And yet this is precisely why we *must* continue to involve ourselves. We need to reclaim the purity of our early values, ideals and concepts and we need to challenge the diluting and compromising of them within present partnership poor practice. We need to nurture better partnerships within the honest and creative conditions that enable them. This now brings us to our 'growing spaces'.

Jackie

I suggested to Julie that we write this book together as I knew I couldn't write it without her! We had worked together for a number of years and it was really through discussions with Julie that my understanding of what it means to work in partnerships took shape. I thought I had a pretty good idea already but soon found that much more was required than I at first thought! It was through a discussion of some reading I had done about 'spaces' and how the idea of space can be used to think about what happens in partnerships that the idea of a 'growing space' took shape. Julie had also built on concepts of using 'space' as a way of considering partnerships, and in our usual manner of tossing about ideas over coffee, we developed and adapted this insight.

We use the concept of 'growing spaces' in this book to understand how partnerships work. A 'growing space' is where working in a partnership is a positive experience for all those in it. This is the opposite of a 'restricted space' where all within a partnership do not find it to be such a positive experience. A restricted space may benefit some but not others, whereas a growing space should benefit and acknowledge all within it. A growing space allows partners to learn together and develop together; a restricted space is where some people are controlled by other people's agendas and egos. This book follows the theme of a garden growing, from the early stages of a partnership ('preparing the ground' and 'sowing the seeds') right through to the development of partnerships, and ends with the 'blossoming' and 'distribution of new growth' to enable further partnerships to flourish. Pests and diseases are always an issue, however, and what these are in the context of partnerships is also explored.

It is entirely fitting that Julie as a community activist and I as an academic should have written this book together. We have tried to model the book in the way that we have worked together and with all the wonderful people who have written about their experiences of what good partnership is. This doesn't mean that we always agree, as that is not the case. What it does mean is that we have always listened to each other and decided jointly how the book should work and be written.

Julie continues

We first created a layout for the growth of partnerships and alliances that our partners addressed through responding to a questionnaire, through structured discussions or through free reflection. Jackie and I then constructed the creative spaces where these ideas could be developed between us as conditions for and stages of good organic growth within human relationships. Partners were further involved in commenting on our writing. This enabled more richness and adaption.

Jackie's persistence and methodical organisation has enabled the 'book within me' to blossom. I would not have made the time to put pen to paper without her. We have been good for one another as partners. And to the best of our abilities, we have jointly tried to nurture the *process* of our writing, as well as its *contents*, into a growing space. My personal hope is that our book will have relevance for any individual or group of people who have genuine passion and yearning to work closely with others in creating growing spaces for themselves.

Jackie concludes

I am the cautious, thoughtful and measured partner and Julie is the more fearless and flamboyant ally. Together, with our collaborators, I think something quite beautiful and moving has been written, and I hope you enjoy our book as well as learn from the wisdom gained from all the contributors to it.

THE PARTNERSHIPS

Advocacy In Action:
a collective of service-user educators and activists who set out to work with anyone wanting to share power[1]

This set of partnerships describes the career of a small service-user group based in Nottingham which comes into being in 1989 when a mixed

---

1   Collaboratively written by Kevin Chettle, Julie Gosling and Brian Pendred, incorporating contributions from *Polly Brown, Mark Lymbery, *Eileen O'Hara, *Anthony Wilde and *Lee Yan (*names changed).

group of citizens with and without learning disabilities starts to question the boxes different people are kept in and to look for better ways to be together, as 'equal quality' people. Their ideas are very radical for the time but catch on to a new wave of change, which transports them to many experiences and opportunities.

By 1992, Advocacy In Action have gained three national honours, including winning the important *Social Work Today's* Equal Opportunities Award 1991, beating 25 local authority contenders. They continue to teach at a number of universities in the UK and are developing service user-led programmes – many years ahead of government imperatives to involve people who use services.

And in 2011, after 21 years, Advocacy In Action remain independent, active and on the front edge of community-led action. Members now include disabled people, homeless and ex-homeless citizens, substance users, carers, Travellers and Gypsies, and older people of diverse ethnicities, all working together across the boundaries that separate them one from another and from more powerful sections of society.

Together they reflect on what they have learned about themselves and others as 'service and systems survivors' through working in partnerships.

The partnerships to watch for are those among service users, within and between different community groups, and between individuals and communities and the practitioners, policy-makers and academics who serve their interests.

A Place to Call our Own (APTCOO): a group of parents who seek better lives, opportunities and services for their disabled children

Trish Green writes:

> My introduction to the world of partnerships began after our daughter Emma was born.
>
> Emma is our third child and a bundle of love, life, laughter and mischief, but when she was born we did not know the treasures and life-changing achievements that she would bring.
>
> Shortly after I gave birth, a doctor came round to see me and asked me to come with him to a side room; he undressed Emma and laid her on a stainless steel table/bench of some sort. He then, without waiting for my husband or any other support, proceeded to describe

'imperfections' of my precious baby. He told me that he had seen a similar baby a few weeks ago and that the baby only lived 48 hours which was a blessing as he would have been 'a cabbage' if he had survived. This was my first taste of partnerships – or lack of it!

Initially I was in a state of shock and went into my 'cave' lonely, confused and isolated. I had to keep strong for the rest of the family and everyone kept telling us how lovely Emma was and how she had all the time in the world to catch up – but I needed more – after a while I started searching for information about Emma's syndrome. In the end we found eight families in different countries with children with the same condition. This was a relief but they were so far away.

The realisation came in the end that actually names of syndromes and 'labels' did not matter, that we loved Emma for who she is and would never want to change her. I needed the support of other families with similar lives, feelings, emotions and issues and I needed to ensure the quality of life both now and in the future for Emma and for the rest of my precious family.

I had slowly and without realising it come out of my cave and had a new zest for life. After restarting work I gained enough confidence to move forward and engage and talk to other parents who lived local to Mansfield with children with all sorts of differing disabilities or needs. I found that we all had that common thread, that need for support information and pathways to services.

APTCOO was set up in 1991 by a group of parents. A small group came together and realised we had so much in common with feelings of worry, isolation, frustration or that our world had changed. People were talking a different language and people came into your life with strange names such as occupational therapists, physiotherapists and who were they and what did they do? Nobody understood our lives and the issues that we faced, even friends and family; although they tried to understand, they didn't quite 'get it'. As a group we found that we could support each other. We didn't want pity and we didn't want pity for our children or our families. What we did want was acceptance of the love and laughter they, our children, brought, and for them to be accepted as children. We wanted to celebrate the individual achievements of our children even though these were different from those of their peers and the things that they did might be seen as different. We had the same need for somewhere we could go with our feelings, emotions and issues – where we could find information, support, access to different services and ways forward. Nobody had told us what services were out there or how we could access them. The organisation grew from here to develop partnerships with parents and their extended families as well as other groups within the voluntary sector, other statutory organisations and funding bodies. Our partnerships with the statutory sector included working with individuals and individual teams within health, education and social care. It also included working at a strategic level in relation to government initiatives in regeneration and safeguarding children.

Asperger's Consultation Group: a partnership of service-user researchers

Jackie writes:

This is a partnership of three adults with Asperger's who are working with me on a piece of research in Nottinghamshire to find out what other adults with Asperger's think about the services that they receive to support them. Duncan McGregor, Katrina Fox and Laura Hickman have worked with me to design a questionnaire, analyse the results and devise and conduct interviews and focus groups with adults with Asperger's. The group meet about once a month and have been meeting for about two years at the time of writing. I facilitate discussions at each session by agreeing with the group what the task for the session is and asking questions and making suggestions that prompt the discussion. It has been the request of the group that I have this role as they are comfortable with this rather than another member taking it on. The possibility of someone else facilitating sessions was discussed early on but the members of the group felt that this would be an unwanted pressure on them and would take away from the enjoyment they get from working in the group. This is interesting as in other settings it would be important to share the responsibility for this task and the power that it gives. However, in this particular case it met the needs of the group far better by me being the facilitator. The group works through having discussions about the particular phase of the research that they are working on together and recording the discussions. Initially the recording was done by writing discussion points up on flipchart paper and then I would type this up, but this changed to the group writing up their thoughts directly onto a laptop and agreeing together that the record is what they want to say. This partnership has had unexpected benefits for all concerned. Although the purpose of the group is to do some research together, and this is in fact what the group is doing, it has given all the members something really positive and significant over and above this. The group has been really important to all the members as everyone has gained in many ways from being a member. Friendships have been formed and trust established among the members. The question of identity is one that is often discussed by the group. People who do not have Asperger's are sometimes called 'neuro typical' and the group sometimes jokingly refer to me as an 'NT'. As an 'NT' I have been really privileged to be a part of very meaningful and personal discussions about what it means to have Asperger's, and I have been delighted that the group members have felt safe enough to have such discussions. The fact that the group regard it as a 'partnership of equals' is testament to how well the group works together. The combination of the opportunity to develop friendships, to develop new skills as researchers but not feel pressured into uncomfortable roles has been key to the success of the group. The freedom to explore what it is to have Asperger's and to be free from the pressure to 'pretend to be neuro typical' has provided the group members with a unique opportunity. From my own perspective, it has been a pure joy to work with Katrina, Duncan and Laura, and they have taught me more than I have taught them. The stereotype of people with Asperger's is that they are unable to empathise and this is often portrayed in the media. What I have found is three people who think very deeply about themselves and also other people and who offer real support and understanding to each other. In fact, many 'NTs' could learn from this group. The group are working on a model of understanding Asperger's from the *inside out*, rather than from the *outside in*, based on information from the research. We hope to present this to key services when the project is finished.

East Midlands Adults PQ Partnership (EMAPP): a forum for course development, delivery and quality assurance

Jackie writes:

EMAPP is a partnership of people representing De Montfort University, service users and carers, six local authorities (Derby City, Nottinghamshire, Northamptonshire, Lincolnshire, Leicester City and Leicestershire) and St Andrews Healthcare. The partnership meets as a Stakeholder Board that governs the post-qualifying (PQ) award for adults' social work. The Board meets quarterly although much work goes on between partners in the times between meetings. This PQ award has been running at De Montfort University in its current form for five years now, and has been developed by all the partners. Candidates who study the award attend teaching days at the University, and workshops that are facilitated in their employing agencies by practice mentor assessors (PMAs). They also have individual support from their PMAs in tutorial and mentoring sessions. Academics as well as service users and carers deliver teaching sessions. All resources for the course have been jointly developed and agreed by all partners concerned, thus ensuring they are academically rigorous as well as relevant, and reflect practitioner and service user and carer perspectives. Candidates are assessed through their written reflections on their work with service users as well as through being observed in their practice with service users, and have to reflect on feedback from their PMAs as well as by the service user or carer with whom they are working. The Stakeholder Board has the role of quality assuring the award as well as making decisions in relation to its development. Meetings are often lively and debate 'hot' as so many different perspectives are represented in the one forum. Agreement on issues is not always speedy, but it does come as all partners are committed to making the award the best it can be and working together in a positive way. The partnership was a finalist in the Skills for Care annual Accolades Awards 2010 that recognised it as an excellent example of partnership working. The partners who have contributed to this book are Larissa Barker, Kevin Chettle, Julie Gosling, Jackie Martin, Mick Wilkinson and Jeanette Wood.

Ed Morecroft and Sarah Craggs: a partnership in training

Ed Morecroft is a service user and Sarah Craggs is a person-centred planning (PCP) trainer who works for Nottinghamshire County Council. Ed reflects:

> We met at a local day service when Sarah was doing a talk on PCP.

Ed thought it was 'a load of old nonsense' and was very mistrustful because he had done things in the past and they had stopped halfway through and he was left with a load of work half done and no support to do any more. Sarah recognised Ed's talents and potential and was keen for him to get involved in helping her to deliver training and tell others about what was possible, but Ed did not believe it:

Sarah said would I help her to deliver PCP training by talking about my plan – this escalated with other people starting to ask me to do things. I became vice-chair of the partnership board – co-chaired conferences, did a 'Tomorrow's Leaders' course, things just exploded – I started to tell that others were listening to me and my confidence grew.

In this book Ed and Sarah discuss how they have worked together and what they have learned from each other, and Ed also reflects on some of his other involvements:

Other people started to help out with training, so we went to Blackpool on a 'Train the Trainers' course and this helped us work together. When we came back we did a person-centred plan…this helped us set goals – we decided that in a year we wanted our own company with £1000 in the bank – it took us three years but after a lot of hard work we set up 'We Can Do It' training.

June Sadd: personal experiences of partnership

June says of herself:

I am a survivor of the psychiatric system and an activist for social justice. I work at national, regional and local levels in social work education. I am from a minority community and have lived in England for most of my life. I have two sons and am absolutely thrilled to have my first granddaughter.

Using my survivor perspective I work at national level in alliances with agencies responsible and accountable for strategy, policy and regulation in social work education. At local and regional levels using a community development approach I work with colleges to develop the involvement of service users and carers in social work education. Much of this work involves working in alliances. I am also a qualified practice educator working with social work students in several colleges in the region; again this role requires working in alliance with other members of the learning team – the student, the practice supervisor and the tutor.

I am a researcher, particularly working with qualitative research involving participatory and emancipatory methodology. The research is commissioned nationally and regionally and is mostly carried out with one or two co-researchers or with a larger research team; both structures involve working in alliance.

The Long Distance Gang:
partners who travel physical, emotional and artistic
journeys while making a film together in Ireland[2]

This partnership describes the planning, making and filming of a journey to Ireland in 2008 and of what happens to the people involved as a result. The commercial film *Arise, You Gallant Sweeneys!* documents a road trip made in late summer by an unusual and memorable band of travellers, some of whom have been away from home for a very, very long time. At the core of the partnership lie the experiences of a group of Irish working 'navvies', who travel to the UK as very young men in the 1960s and never make it home. The original Long Distance Gangs have worked and tramped the length and breadth of Britain for over half a century – part of the huge workforce that builds the power stations, the motorways, the bridges, the great public buildings and sprawling council estates. But what happens to the men who build the motorways when they reach the end of the road? Although many return to Ireland, and others find a good life in England, there are still numerous casualties – too proud to share the pain or to ask for help, too ashamed to try to get back home again. Older now and fragile, some have tramped a harsh thankless life; some have slept rough on the streets. Many need and choose to drink alcohol.

A group of older drinkers – Tom Coffey, Pat Kelly, Sean Travers Lynch, Joe McGrory and Tom Sweeney – plan a journey in company with Irish friends, community artists, film-makers and with wider support from staff in their care homes. We follow as they embark on a rambling, emotional and ultimately celebratory visit back to families, villages and dreams left behind a generation before. As they retrace their steps, new and long forgotten narratives begin to unfold. The Gang's journey brings people briefly back to their birth places after absences of up to 50 years, and its story captures the mixed feelings and experiences the journey throws up for everyone. But what is created is not a film *about* the men; it is a film *by* them. It is therefore unique in that the group retain directorial and collective ownership over all the material produced and, indeed, total autonomy in all aspects of

---

2   Collaboratively written by Julie Gosling, Dave Milburn and Ian Nesbitt, incorporating contributions from Tom Coffey (RIP), Pat Kelly, Joe McGrory, Sean Travers Lynch (RIP) and other residents and care staff at 32 Bentinck Road ('32').

the journey. The Long Distance Gang (named after their shared working history) have many experiences; among them are construction workers, musicians, film-makers, activists, housing and care workers, and survivors of orphanages, care systems, street homelessness, alcohol dependency, sectarian and domestic violence and mental health problems.

Within the partnership, however, there are no labels – no 'volunteers' or 'clients', no 'carers', 'experts' or 'vulnerable people', no 'alcoholics' or 'pioneers' – just a group of people who agree to plan a journey together, travel together, and make a film together, and the wider partners who engage with them. The empowering impact on everyone's well-being and dignity is profound. It proves a joyous and grounding experience for all involved in making or supporting the journey and the ensuing film affects everyone who sees it.

The journey takes place in 2008 and partnership continues still. The Long Distance Gang moves on to work with communities and with learners and educators. They learn how to market and sell their filmed experiences as DVDs.

The partnerships to watch out for are those within the band of travellers who make it to Ireland, those between the travellers and the care system surrounding some of them, and later, between the traveller/film-makers and those seeking to associate themselves with the success of the film. Some participants are now dead but they live on irrepressibly within the experiences created by this remarkable alliance.

The Long Distance Gang create a true growing space where people unite as mutual supporters, explorers and discoverers, mutual storytellers and creators.

My Final Journey:
the last months of life[3]

This partnership describes the end stages in the life of Sean Travers Lynch, one of The Long Distance Gang, whose death in February 2011 marks an eight-month final journey led by Sean. In fulfilling many of his end-of-life wishes, wise or 'less wise', and defining a very personal

---

3   Collaboratively written by Julie Gosling, Dave Milburn, Ian Nesbitt and Sean
     Travers Lynch (RIP), incorporating contributions from Pat Kelly, Mick Regan
     and other residents and care staff at '32'.

notion of well-being and the informal sources of support that enable it, Sean and partners resist more medical models of palliative care and ultimately enable a peaceful and dignified death 'at home' in a Nottingham residential alcohol management unit for older men ('32'), surrounded by friends and family.

Sean describes himself as 'a working-man-tramp' and a big drinking man. He vehemently insists that he will 'never change' – moreover, does not *want* to change. This throws out big challenges to those who would curb his challenging lifestyle and tidy up his dying. And it also throws a spanner in the end-of-life conveyor belt that carts people off to the places that dying people are expected to inhabit.

Within this partnership there are lots of good and passionate intentions around 'what is best' for people. The strength of the alliance is Sean himself at its centre, guiding, challenging and inspiring everyone around him. The respect of partners is characterised by the willingness with which people are prepared to lay aside their own strong values and be led by Sean's wishes, regardless of how 'appropriate' they might be deemed.

The alliance brings out the best in everyone and in particular highlights the crucial role of other older residents as peer supporters and enablers, the flexibility and openness to change of care staff, and furthermore, the purity and independence of community advocacy which digs its heels in to insist that Sean's personal blueprint for living and dying remains at the centre at all times.

Sean makes a final return visit to Ireland in December 2010, eight weeks before his death, accompanied by Julie and Ian Nesbitt ('Nes'), two friends from the earlier journey in 2008 as members of the erstwhile Long Distance Gang. Between the three of them they make health-related decisions and manage pain control in Ireland as a united team, while enabling and celebrating the wildest sweetest songs within Sean's heart. The lovely winding lanes of childhood memories are retraced back to the village school, the church, the deep still lake where father fished with son. Sean recalls holding the 'big man's' hand – as he stands once again at the water's edge, now gripping onto the hands of his friends.

On return to England, renewed and hopeful, Sean plans to make it back to Ireland once more in the spring. However, cancer waits for no one, and as he starts to weaken again, the care home makes a decision to move Sean to a local hospice. This is the last place he wants to be. Anxious and fearful, but unable to make himself understood, it is up to

Sean's community advocates to fight his corner and insist that his final wishes be honoured. Support from an inspiring professional partner – the care home manager – quickly puts into place the extra provisions, the Macmillan nurses, Crossroads carers and of course, the funding that will enable Sean's return. And so it is that Sean comes back to spend his final days in his room at '32'.

It is now the other residents, all older drinking men too, who become the big force within the partnership, sharing the final days with Sean in much the way they did before he became so poorly – beer cans and fags on the go and memories spilling out along the way. Sean, by this stage, can neither drink nor smoke, but is still able to enjoy his comrades' pleasures.

Sean dies peacefully in the arms of the daughter whom he had lost for most of her childhood and later life. All partners then work hard to support her in planning his burial and in raising the money to enable a funeral of choice. It is the film of the 2008 Ireland journey that brings in the necessary income, when shown in local pubs and community centres. The funeral itself is characterised by the visible presence of all partners – community advocates, friends, family, care staff and the older residents, humble, dignified and courageous in Sean's wake.

The partnerships to watch for are the bonds between Sean and his chosen community supporters, their alliances and/or conflicts with formal care staff and management, and the strong links of shared experience between Sean and the other older residents. The growing spaces in this partnership are inhabited by the living and the dying, and show us how to create truly person-centred practice.

Older People's Partnership Services (OPPS): partnerships with older service-user researchers and older people receiving care and support[4]

This partnership describes the planning, delivery and results of a peer-led action research programme commissioned by Leicester City Council

---

4   Written by Julie Gosling, incorporating contributions from Michael Gilhooley, Ron Hayward, Carol King, Mary McCausland, Amita Naik, Reshma Patel, Anne Purcell, Jullette Ruddock, Chandrika Singh and Joyce Willard, representing the OPPS group and Leicester City Council.

in 2009, where a self-selected team of people, aged from 60 to 83, learn about research, set up an investigative framework – together with the values and benchmarks underpinning it – and engage with a diverse range of older people in receipt of home care, whose ages span from 68 to 91. Leicester is an ethnically diverse city and this is reflected both in the research team and their subjects.

The research is developed and supported by a service-user consultant from Advocacy In Action working closely with a service manager from Leicester City Council to establish the process-led partnership that enables older people to rediscover, renew and develop skills, confidence and capacity. The research group itself, however, remains autonomous and becomes so enthusiastic that it sets up an independent organisation committed to the rights, interests and requirements of older people. OPPS pledges to work in partnership both with local communities of older people and with the agencies that provide services to them.

The OPPS research programme proves a compelling and successful partnership that unlocks the previously silent voices of older and vulnerable care receivers in the city. The research findings do not always make comfortable reading, and impose some unavoidable and urgent requirements on both the local authority and the care services they commission from local agencies. The 2010 launch of the findings and recommendations to Leicester politicians, managers and providers is a powerful and emotional event, led by the older researchers and some of their research participants – leaving the professional audience in tears. The presence and voices of people in their 80s and 90s, the simplicity of their wishes and the eloquence of their often painful testimonies demand humane, genuine engagement and action. Leicester City Council recognises its responsibilities within this partnership, not only listening to the OPPS recommendations but also formally adopting them.

The OPPS group is commissioned in late 2010, despite a stringent financial climate, to work in partnership with Leicester City Council to develop and implement the required action plan, and further funding is extended in 2011 as the growing importance of the OPPS model is taken on board – older people engaging with other older people and making decisions in partnership with the decision-makers and providers who serve them.

The group itself changes, with various original members moving on to other partnership activities within the authority and community. But their vacant places in OPPS are taken up by some of the older research subjects, who, having been inspired by their involvement, are now hungry for more!

At the point of writing, the group are developing training and awareness programmes, led by older people, to enhance the standard of support and care services locally. And they are working closely with politicians and service leads on the many areas where local authority policy and OPPS ideas, vision and strategies have a close fit.

The partnerships to watch for are those between the older researchers themselves, their engagement with the older people they interview, the interface between OPPS and the service-user consultant and her facilitators, and its partnerships – both formal and informal – with Leicester City Council together with its commissioned providers.

Our Promise to Act (PAct): service-user authors and activites reflect on partnership[5]

This partnership describes an alliance that has grown during the putting together of this book.

As we progress with writing up the partnerships, it becomes apparent that a separate space is required where service-user participants can freely describe their experiences – positive or negative – of service-user collaboration with service providers and or educators, without compromising their position or that of their allies within the other partnerships they belong to, that are also discussed in the book. PAct is therefore a discussion and writing alliance to explore general experiences of working in formal partnerships within statutory and academic forums and working groups.

The members of PAct all share concerns over the way partnership is presently progressing within health and social care and honestly desire, without offence, to draw attention to what really works or does not work

---

5   Collaboratively written by Kevin Chettle, Julie Gosling and *Anil Kapur, incorporating reflections from Gina Hardesty, Nasira Patel, Reshma Patel and others (*name changed).

for service-user and carer participants. PAct associates recognise that they have a freedom that professional colleagues are not always granted – to speak their minds without necessarily compromising their roles or security.

PAct promises to act, in that the people within it have pledged to try and make a real difference within their present and future partnerships – or withdraw if necessary. These particular explorations are solely from a service-user perspective, and identify some of the questions that service users are now beginning to ask. There is within the reflections both celebration of good practice and a real challenge to move partnership on.

The PAct partnership exists only within the putting together of this book, although its individual members can be found within the other alliances, named or anonymous.

React: disabled and non-disabled children working together through performance, movement and music

Kara Robinson writes:

Beaufort School is a small, 42-place school in Birmingham for primary-aged pupils with cognition and learning disabilities. Beaufort School and Colebourne Primary School co-located in 2008 and have developed a range of formal and informal opportunities for their pupils to work, play and learn together. One of the most important aims of the two-school partnership is for both groups of children to learn from one another and for the wider community to share in this experience.

In 2010 Colebourne Primary School took part in a Creative Partnerships project sponsored by Bright Space. Fourteen pupils from the two co-located schools worked to develop and perform an inclusive dance and multimedia project. The project provided opportunities for children with physical and learning disabilities to work with their peers from mainstream education in an equal, empowering and meaningful way. The pupils selected from Beaufort School were those who found it difficult to communicate and work in a way that was understood by their peers from Colebourne. For example, they were not yet able to communicate verbally or by using a formal communication system such as Makaton signing. The chosen pupils from Colebourne Primary were selected because they found it difficult to interact with their disabled peers due to their attitude toward them. The aim was for the pupils to learn from one another and to share their experiences with the wider community; they were to be equal partners.

Clare Reynolds and Paul Rogerson were selected to work as creative partners to facilitate the process. Clare used dance techniques to develop a mutual language between the pupils, while Paul enhanced the pupils' ability to express themselves through the use of assistive technology and multimedia. The creative process took the form of daily workshops over a period of several weeks. These sessions provided the pupils with opportunities to gain understanding of one another, to develop work as partners and individually, to express themselves through dance and empower one another by communicating in new ways.

The creative partners developed a final piece to showcase the work that the pupils had produced. This was called *React* as it focused on the pupils reacting to each other, as well as the music, lights and images on stage which were triggered by the movements made by the pupils. A *Soundbeam®*, a device which converts movement into electrical information, was used to trigger video clips made by the pupils as they moved across the stage. *Khoros®* (designed by Paul Rogerson), a device which controls lights and sounds as different panels are touched, was used to perform music as chosen by the pupils live on stage. *React* was performed in several venues across the city, including Birmingham Town Hall.

One of the best outcomes of the project was the friendships that were forged between the pupils from both schools. Pupils were given the opportunity to work equally in partnership, rather than the pupils from Colebourne 'helping' the pupils from Beaufort. Kara Robinson was a teacher involved in the project and she has written about it for this book. This project took place in 2010.

Reshma Patel and Sherma Patel: a partnership in social work learning and teaching

Reshma Patel is a disabled service-user consultant and Sherma Patel is a senior lecturer at De Montfort University. Reshma undertook a module at De Montfort University which enabled her to then go on to assess qualifying students on the Social Work degree. Sherma supported Reshma in this module and acted as her PMA; this meant that they met regularly to discuss Reshma's learning and progress on the module. They describe this process as a 'roller-coaster journey' as it had some very difficult aspects initially, but grew into a strong partnership as the two women learned to trust each other.

Stephen Vickers:
best-interest partnerships with people
deemed to lack capacity

Stephen Vickers is a qualified social worker, an approved mental health professional and an independent best-interest assessor. He project-managed the development and implementation of both the Mental Health Act 2007 and the Deprivation of Liberty Safeguards (DoLS) across Leicester City, Leicestershire and Rutland before going on to manage the DoLS service until August 2011.

Stephen is a visiting lecturer at De Montfort University, the University of Leicester and the University of Birmingham. He has received professional recognition as a lead in best practice with regard to the Mental Capacity Act and the DoLS. He has been a key speaker at several national conferences, including 'Putting the Mental Capacity Act into Practice' (Social Care Institute for Excellence), 'A Focus on Best Practice in Serious Case Reviews in Adults' (East Midlands Joint Improvement Partnership) and 'Mental Capacity Act and Deprivation of Liberty Safeguards – a National Conference Exploring Developments in Practice, Case Law and Inspection' (Royal College of Psychiatrists).

Stephen also continues to work as an independent best interest assessor. The role requires him to undertake assessments within a legal framework for people over the age of 18 who have a mental disorder. This includes an assessment of a person's mental capacity in making decisions about care or treatment in hospitals or care homes when circumstances amounting to deprivation of liberty are required to provide such care.

Stephen writes:

Best interest assessments under the Deprivation of Liberty Safeguards go to the very heart of citizenship and human rights and involve complex decision-making processes that are set against strict and tight statutory time frames. Central to all decision-making is the involvement of service users and their carers. Forming partnerships quickly in the assessment process is critical in order to safeguard each service user's human rights, their dignity and in ensuring the best possible outcome is achieved for those involved.

Stephen believes that those who may fall under the DoLS are among the most vulnerable of adults. He writes:

> ...best interest decisions under the framework of the Mental Capacity Act are not substitute decisions. The outcome therefore may not necessarily be one that the service user agrees with. It is at this point that the nature of that person's vulnerability is most exposed.

Stephen admits that at least part of his passion for this line of work is inspired by the personal circumstances of his grandmother who herself lost capacity in several important areas of her life after developing a dementia-related illness. Further motivation comes from a firm belief in the foundations of social work values, including a passion for partnership and problem-solving in human relationships that empowers and liberates people to ultimately enhance their well-being.

Chapter **1**

PREPARING THE GROUND

MOTIVATION

Partnerships are formed for different reasons and from different motivations. The nature of how and why people come together defines the relationships they build. Some partnerships are voluntary; others are not. Some are time-limited and some are open-ended; some relatively new, while others have been around for a long time. Sometimes people or organisations seek one another out with shared purpose. Other types of alliances are forged from relationships between people who share a passion for human rights. These partnerships may themselves extend further to seek professional and political ties in order to influence practice and thinking. Sometimes bonds are forced on people when others intervene in their lives. Still other unions spring from the desire of some to help and improve the lot of others who in turn look for assistance or support. When all within the partnership share some unity of purpose or vision, the road ahead and the horizon may seem clear. But where individuals or organisations are thrown together, the challenge is to make the best use of the territory and the opportunities that partnership opens up.

People coming together don't always define or even recognise the mutual terrain. Advocacy In Action (see p.17) recall getting together in 1989: 'We don't see ourselves as a partnership or as anything special – we are just a group who are fed up with the way some of us get put away in boxes because we are different.'

Some people can't accept the word 'partnership'. Life experiences within The Long Distance Gang (see p.24), for instance, give many homeless men a shared deep mistrust of people. Owning any sense or shape of agreed togetherness does not happen overnight – a haphazard coming together and being together is often down to chance. The word 'partnership' arrives much later in the story as the group embarks on a rambling road trip to film their return to villages, homes and dreams left behind up to half a century before in Southern Ireland.

June Sadd (see p.23) prefers the term 'alliance' rather than 'partnership' as she believes this term better addresses the fact that there are often power differentials and imbalances in many partnerships, particularly between service users and professionals. An alliance allows for this disparity in power more than a partnership approach.

Anil Kapur, Our Promise to Act (PAct) (see p.29) member, describes some of his partnerships:

> As a disabled service-user consultant, I have worked with universities, where we have enjoyed great relationships, and made all sorts of partnership plans for the future, which then fail to materialise. I feel that sometimes the university's story and my story do not match up. So I would like to use my experience here to better represent the realities of some of the associations we have built, as I see them.
>
> Professionals make quite a lot of our 'partnerships'. But I maintain that the relationships are sometimes not yet a partnership in the true sense of the word. It has been to date about people engaged in completing a task. My role has *not* always been to challenge. Sometimes the only choice remaining for me is whether or not to cooperate. This is not an equal relationship in my eyes. It is everyone else that has started to redefine these relationships with the latest buzzword – 'partnership!'

Some recognise the tensions and contradictions in the term 'partnership', and they seek to reclaim the word by unpicking and challenging the control hiding within. The Older People's Partnership Services (OPPS) (see p.27), for example, sets out a clear definition and principles for its dealings with local authorities and other partner agencies.

PAct recognises that the P-word is often used to embody a *commitment* to a principle. But it is in practice that its diverse meanings for academics, service users and practitioners begin to unfold.

Perhaps the idea of commitment best summarises the flux of understandings and contributions in the East Midlands Adults PQ Partnership (EMAPP) (see p.21). There is here a genuine and commendable *wanting to* work together.

Partnerships don't just *happen*; they are often nurtured by one or two key people. For example, the Asperger's Consultation Group (see p.20) grows through the effort of a university lecturer and researcher, Jackie Martin, gathering the views and experience of people with Asperger's syndrome. Preserving and celebrating the hidden stories of Irish migrants is a passion shared by Julie Gosling and Ian Nesbitt ('Nes'), an artist and community film-maker, and it is their early conversations that lead to a gathering of older Irish men who need and choose to drink. The OPPS group develops from a chance conversation, when local authority service manager Mary McCausland and Julie Gosling bump into one another at a meeting. EMAPP, on the other hand, has a formal organisational remit to build up and operate through partnerships, while PAct evolves through the writing of this book.

Members of Advocacy In Action are originally introduced to one another by a social work assistant, although individuals then come together as a rights group by choice. Advocacy In Action recalls:

> ...we are not *set up* by others – no steering group, funders, advisers, or enablers – we have nothing at the beginning – no money, no qualifications, no confidence – just the energy born from anger and frustration and wanting change – and this huge, huge belief in one another and in what we might achieve together – we have no direction – no big plans – no targets or agendas – these come later as we grow more confident and realise we have skills. At the start we just want to meet as a group so that we can speak out about our lives.

Regardless of why partnerships are formed, the *motivations* of the people within them are important in determining their effectiveness. Motivation may be something that is easier to see in partnerships that are entered into voluntarily.

Older people give many individual reasons for joining OPPS – promoting services, strengthening existing forums, peer togetherness, having a moan at the council, wanting to escape loneliness, giving something back, telling their personal stories, being useful and feeling valued, having a chance of personal status and power. But a common desire of all participants is to make life better for older people. Similarly, the members of the Asperger's Consultation Group say they get involved because they want to 'make a difference', to use their life experience for the benefit of others, to promote the understanding of others and show that Asperger's could be 'used for something positive.' It is important for the Asperger's Consultation Group that they are able to join together to work positively and can be 'active rather than passive'.

Advocacy In Action's early motives stand the course of time:

> We want to make good spaces where people can be together and feel confident and proud, voice anger at unfair treatment, speak out for what we need and wish for, and feel safe to be ourselves as we are, without apologising, staying out of sight or trying to fit in or change to please others. We are happy to work with anyone who wants to nurture and share positive power.

When some pupils at Colebourne Primary and Beaufort Primary find it difficult to build relationships between the schools through a lack of either understanding or acceptance, a positive response is developed to support integration. The *React* project expresses motivation in terms of what it aims to achieve:

> Beaufort School is co-located with Colebourne Primary, in Hodge Hill, Birmingham. Our aim is to work together to promote a fully inclusive, accepting and empowering environment for pupils at both schools, creating meaningful opportunities for children to work and play together.

Both schools want to tackle relationship issues between pupils through supported, motivating and fun activities which children take part in together:

> The first aim of our partnership is to promote positive relationships with an understanding of pupils' strengths and individuality from both schools. The second aim is to build opportunities for interactive, creative and independent expression, while raising the pupils' profile within the wider community.

EMAPP convenes for the specific purpose of ensuring that an academic programme for qualified social workers and other allied professionals provides a good learning experience for all who undertake the course:

> ...the partnership is seen as an essential element of defining academic, agency and service-user expectations for the PQ programme. It is anticipated that joint responsibility for all aspects will result in a high-quality programme that provides better outcomes for people who use these services.

Formal expressions of partnership look forward to what is hoped will follow. But do they foresee all the tangled motivations, hopes and commitments that spring up? Nevertheless, EMAPP's inception conveys the absolute spirit of *wanting* partnership to prosper and to blossom.

The OPPS collaboration develops from a research proposal. Leicester City Council seeks older people's views on a new outcome-based home care pilot and wants a service-user consultant. Advocacy In Action wants to ensure that the voices of older people are heard and that new services are a true response to people's stated needs and wishes. They also want older people to have the chance to become researchers and plan the evaluation. Older participants are so enthusiastic that they decide to start their own group to help the Council in many different ways. And so OPPS takes on a life of its own and the older researchers become co-producers.

Julie Gosling, for PAct, considers a university/practitioner/service-user research partnership that sets out to study the effectiveness of service-user involvement in social work teaching. And it has to be said again that there are many agendas operating at the beginning of this partnership – from organisational aims such as 'getting published' and 'creating academic capital' to building up capacity and promoting the voices and choices of people who use services. Accessing funding is another end, as is the pursuit of excellence in teaching and practice. These agendas are not all declared openly from the outset. But from the beginning there is, nevertheless, a shared willingness from all to work together in 'new and exciting ways' and to 'involve new people'. How will moving from principle to practicalities test this willingness?

Reshma Patel and Sherma Patel's partnership (see p.31) is formed in order to support Reshma to successfully complete an academic qualification which she can go on to use in assessing social work students on a qualifying programme at De Montfort University. But as Reshma is a student and Sherma her mentor and assessor, there are power differences in their relationship. So this is not regarded as a partnership at the outset, although it becomes one as a relationship and trust develop.

Their mutual driver is to work together. Reshma wants to successfully complete the qualification so she can be an assessor for the University. She is committed to learn and draw on her own experience. Sherma's motivation is two-fold. She aims to 'enable Reshma to meet her objectives' and furthermore 'to work with a person that uses services in a different way and to achieve a different relationship.' For Sherma it is important that she 'doesn't come in as a social worker/assessor but as someone who recognises their different but equal knowledge bases.'

Ed Morecroft and Sarah Craggs's partnership (see p.22) developed when Sarah sees in Ed real potential. Even though Ed has been let down in the past, he is prepared to take the risk working in partnership with Sarah: 'We meet at a local day service when Sarah does a talk on PCP (person-centred planning)'. Ed thinks it 'a load of old nonsense' and is very mistrustful because he has done things in the past and they have stopped halfway through and he is left with a load of work half done and no support to do any more. Sarah recognises Ed's talents and potential and is keen for him to get involved in helping her to deliver training and tell others about what is possible, but Ed does not believe it.

Belief in one another is essential for growth within partnership. The strong bonds between Sean Travers Lynch and Julie Cassidy Gosling, rooted in the 2008 Long Distance Gang's Ireland adventure, form a platform of belief on which community volunteers and care staff convene together in 2010, as Sean takes charge of and plans towards his imminent death. The partnership is dictated by the rapid advance of Sean's cancer and is often reactive in how it is managed, but its inception is firmly rooted in that first shared journey and in the confidence and strength that original partners now draw from their early success. Everyone has different hopes about what can and indeed *should* be achieved by working towards a 'person-centred' death.

Dave Milburn, manager at '32', describes '...a dignified and progressive state of affairs which requires much energy at times – and not either at the expense of the other residents, nor the running of the home.' All try to respect that Sean's wishes remain paramount, even where they challenge conventional notions of 'well-being' and those medically driven, rigid and risk-wary procedures that continue to dominate institutional care. There are many tensions and emotions to own and live with, as partners passionately state what they feel is the 'best way forward'. The undercurrent of feelings runs strong and uncharted. But perhaps the single true shared vision is that everyone wants to do their part and to be part of this journey, as we travel Sean's final months together.

Trish Green's motivation in setting up A Place to Call our Own (APTCOO) (see p.18) is to do the best for her family and to find like-minded people who can work together with her to influence services for children with disabilities and their families. Her story begins where:

> ...as a parent/carer I feel very isolated and I feel the need to develop partnerships with individuals who understand my feelings, emotions and struggles. I also feel the need for information for support for my child and to help me understand and plan for our future as a family. As I don't know people in a similar situation, my initial concern is for my own family.

Trish remembers, as a parent, recognising the need to develop good relationships with statutory agencies in order to obtain practical support for her daughter Emma to ensure her health and well-being. She also acknowledges the need to develop relationships with other parents. She recalls her early emotions: '...nobody really understands mine and my family's feelings. I feel that we are living in a different world that others don't understand.' Trish's motivation remains to ensure that at all times professionals *do* understand and involve those with experience in decisions that affect their lives.

But where people are assessed as not having the understanding or capacity to make their own decisions, it becomes a challenge to consider any notion of 'partnership' with those who must act on their behalf.

It is certainly not a situation that the person being assessed has chosen, so how can it be considered as 'partnership'? The answer, social worker Stephen Vickers suggests (see p.32), lies in the motivation of the person doing the assessing. If the relationship has any chance of being in the spirit of partnership then the assessor has to be motivated to do everything possible to work in the best interests of the person they are assessing:

> We must quickly forge a relationship with them. Their circumstances, in that they lack capacity, will result in a 'best interest decision' being made on their behalf. We must take into account all factors relevant to the person in a hope to achieve a meaningful relationship with them. It is important to quickly establish a way of communicating so that they can still be involved in the decision-making process. It is also important to remember that even where a person lacks capacity to make the decision for themselves, they will often have views on issues that affect the decision and have views on what outcome they would prefer. The ultimate outcome is to try and make a decision that is in their 'best interests' and their involvement in this process can help to work this out.

In summary

We already have the seeds of exploitation and tokenism identified by Anil and June. The 'community-grown' alliances – Advocacy In Action and APTCOO – are characterised by an organic development, determined independence and desire for change, while partnerships that started from more planned intentions, such as *React* (see p.30) and EMAPP (see p.21), contain a mixture of motivations and power relationships.

People have different motives for being in partnerships – to work together, to challenge, to change things – but to create a true growing space, people must be committed to working together in an honest, positive and inclusive way. And when this happens, the conditions for partnership are ripe.

ALL WELCOME IN THIS PARTNERSHIP!

Is it stating the obvious that people like to feel welcome when they gather together? But welcome greetings and introductions are often hasty or overlooked in the rush to get on with the 'real business'. Advocacy In Action restate an early principle: 'We do not come to work to make machines – we work together to make *people!*' The Asperger's Consultation Group value the warmth and 'humanness' which blossoms from ensuring everyone is made to feel wanted and a part of the group. It is sad but true that there are other gatherings where this does not happen, however.

The uncertainty caused as 'newcomers' join The Long Distance Gang meetings is easily put to rest as the younger film-makers with their shocks of dark hair and beards are jokingly told to 'listen and learn from the grey-heads!' The group includes musicians and artists, storytellers and drinkers, community volunteers and older Irish migrants. Experiences include survival of care systems, rural poverty, child labour, sectarian violence, mental and spiritual distress and work on the large construction sites of Britain. For those partners of shared Irish origin it is easy to be encircled by the warmth, nostalgia and camaraderie, but there is a real Irish welcome for all.

Cancer is never a welcome partner, and when Sean's cancer spreads to his mouth in 2010, some of the helpers who follow in its wake are unwanted too, but necessary, for as Sean's health deteriorates, he needs specialist interventions and increased support with daily living. Sean hates the constraints cancer places on his lifestyle and on his stubborn independence. His demands on the incoming experts bring them to suspect that there are maybe other ways of working. Sean's chosen partners, meanwhile, have to make space for these newcomers, learn to welcome what is needed, and with some tact, nudge the rest away.

Traditional values of courtesy and respect are lived principles for older people at OPPS meetings, where the hand of greeting is extended across racial and cultural boundaries to ensure people are not left out. Principles are translated into a written practical checklist, to ensure everyone feels able to join in at their own pace and to experience themselves as accepted and valued. OPPS meetings always start with a sharing space for members to bring their news, experiences, feelings and gossip to the group. This is popular and significant; it serves as a reminder that older voices, first and foremost, are what OPPS stands for.

PAct members have encountered different ideas – not always compatible – about who should 'belong' within certain groups. As a tension may exist between required quality outcomes and a more process-led focus on capacity-building and involvement, so the value of individuals may be measured less on what they bring or are assumed to bring and more on what is perceived to be required. PAct experience suggests that not all members may be made to feel equally welcome by those within the group who are purely output-focused.

In summary

Sean identifies and resists attempts to colonise his health condition and the paths he should take. PAct warns against those partnerships that seek to 'professionalise' all participants.

Getting to know people as people and valuing them as unique individuals creates an environment where partnerships can develop. Whether engagement is between two individuals or within a group of participants, this sense of warmth between members nurtures the communication and activity that takes place within true growing spaces, as EMAPP's welcome to all and the laid-down principles of OPPS demonstrate.

This should not be confused with those *token* partnerships, where individuals pay mere lip service through bland empty phrases to one another's well-being, while disregarding them in any deeper caring sense, or to the easy complacency where participants *collude* with, or are afraid to challenge, each other. As the partnerships described here open themselves up to readers, they begin to reveal the genuine warmth and engagement, together with an ability to challenge appropriately and respectfully, which nurture real success.

A SPACE TO BE OURSELVES

Experiences within PAct suggest that partners in more formalised settings may not always feel completely comfortable with one another. An 'output pressure' means that colleagues do not routinely invest the time needed to get to know one another as 'people first'.

Partners in the journey through Sean's final months reflect that:

> In some respects, we are limited in this space. Sean can't be 'the law unto himself' as ever before. Julie feels constrained by Sean's illness and his growing difficulties. Dare she be as 'in your face' with a dying man as with that strong brash rebel of Ireland 2008? Workers are torn between professional attitudes as care-givers and more human responses. We are all treading very carefully around one another.

The older people of OPPS and their supporters meet in Leicester Town Hall and in the local authority offices:

> We feel respected and valued in these formal places by the comforts and the courtesy accorded to us. But we are not intimidated by our surroundings – we feel free to be ourselves, relax and take the time to talk about what *we* feel is important. And talk we do! We spend the time we need to get to know one another and feel safe about working together.

The Asperger's Consultation Group feel it important that they are able to contribute in ways that don't pressurise them. They feel able to be themselves and not have to 'pretend to be neuro typical'. To feel 'allowed to be who you are' and not to 'feel put on' enables members to contribute in ways that feel comfortable to them. It is achieved by talking openly about how people want to work together right at the beginning of coming together. No assumptions are made about what roles individuals should have within the group, and this lack of pressure is very important for people. Participants can contribute according to their skills and, even more importantly, feel they can say they don't want to do anything they feel uncomfortable with. Not only do members feel they can truly be themselves, but at the same time, they experience safety in the group and in the knowledge that 'the onus is on the partnership and not on the individual.' A member expresses that, 'I feel like I can contribute without everyone pinning it all on me.' This blend of being free to be themselves but at the same time feeling safe within a group makes partnership a positive experience for all those within it.

The Long Distance Gang's older Irish men are initially reluctant in proposing ideas about how to be together, but soon decide they want to be in a group with people they know, that the freedom to drink and smoke is important, and that they will only talk if and when they feel like it. Meetings will be more about being together than doing tasks. An odd tune or occasional song will not be out of place; rough humour and the 'Craic' are a must! Meetings cannot all be private from care staff but *will not* be discussed behind the men's backs. A record of activity is important 'in *our* language, not care home language.' All partners need steering away from labels that put distance between us — 'workers', 'residents', 'clients', 'vulnerable', 'helpless', 'alcoholics', 'pioneers'. Minutes of discussions will remind people of what makes us laugh and cry, and what we believe in, as well as what we agree to do together.

An excerpt from The Long Distance Gang's meetings log gives a taste:

> We practise for Ireland by driving out to Matlock. Tom uses a cash machine for the first time in his life — 'Holy Mother of God! Would You Look at the Ten Pound Note Coming Out the Wall!' — then there's a five-minute walk and we all help one another, as we don't have too many good legs between us. Pat feels like a drink so we take one in the fresh air in a nearby beer garden with all the witty comments flying around like grit off a workman's shovel. Tom needs proper boots to travel in because he's lost his toes with the frostbite and the previous home just stuffed paper in the gaps.
>
> The older men vote with their feet when they have had enough of a meeting. People stop talking, or start their own conversations, or head for the door. There is still some sense of 'us' and 'them'.

The Long Distance Gang's younger partners say it is important that they aren't seen as 'staff' or 'helpers', or expected to make all the suggestions, or do all the work. People agree it is central that everyone feels comfortable and free to be ourselves, that we get rid of as many labels as possible, and that we all look after one another within the partnership and within the spaces we create together as a group.

Julie reflects with Nes that:

> ...the partnership has to be first and foremost about carving out a space of shared autonomy, choice and safety and about seeding many ideas within that space, to be jointly considered and developed. The openness of the space, with its lack of rigid imported agendas, invites no *passive* response, but an active consideration by participants, of a limitless range of possibilities generated when we ask of ourselves, that cliff-hanger of a question − 'what if?' − and dare to explore the alternatives.

In summary

Members of the Asperger's Consultation Group are very clear about the pressures, stereotypes and expectations that they wish to steer clear of. And The Long Distance Gang was determined not to be incorporated into the processes and language of the formal care system within which this lovely growing space has evolved.

People need to feel respected for who they are. A growing space is created where people are honest with and respectful of one another and speak a language that everyone understands and feels validated by. Then the space is truly owned by all.

GETTING THINGS AGREED AT THE START

When partnerships are entered into, it is important as far as possible to discuss how people within it will work together. For Ed and Sarah this is about being honest about both of their needs and working on trusting each other.

In terms of working together, the most important thing Ed needs to hear is that the support will not collapse as it has done before, so Sarah feels a commitment to follow through, come what may. If the department changes its approach, Sarah will still commit to support Ed:

> We also need to work at developing trust so that we can challenge each other and be honest about how we think things are going − for

example, saying when an exercise has worked or not, when we feel we may have overstepped the mark in terms of humour, when we feel we are in danger of losing the values we share in training.

In working to Sean Travers' final wishes, there are disagreements between partners. Nothing is ever written down formally, but the 'care' standards which collide, cooperate and sometimes come into conflict are Sean's personal blueprint for living and dying, Julie's person-centred advocacy principles, '32's' organisational health and social care requirements and many individual values, hopes and fears.

It is The Long Distance Gang partners who lay the foundations for Sean's final journey, three years previously, when we agree and sign our names to principles for working together on a road trip home to Ireland after long absences. Everyone in the group promises to try to turn up to meetings, to take responsibility for making the trip happen, to stick to agreements, to say when we disagree or are unhappy with decisions, to build up belief in ourselves and in one another, to always look out for positives, to look out for one another's interests, to the well-being of the group as a whole, to turn obstacles into openings, and to always see the opportunities inside of the risks. The provision to be able to disagree with and feel free to challenge one another, without causing injury or offence, is particularly important, although it is hard to realise.

A simple set of statements and promises are set down. Everyone has their own copy and signs it. This proves critical when, miles away from home, familiar boundaries are dissolving within unknown spaces. These early promises override strong individual motivations to go separate ways in Ireland and helps to keep partners safely together.

For Reshma and Sherma the negotiation of how they will work together felt formal at the outset:

> We set up a meeting where we talk about roles, responsibilities and expectations of each other. Within that discussion the values we share are more implicit than explicit. We are still a little bit nervous of each other at this point and so discussions are quite formalised and structured. We share a little about knowledge.

Sherma says what she can provide, in terms of knowledge of the module and requirements, while Reshma says where she thinks her experience will best be utilised.

We have a discussion about agencies that might be appropriate for Reshma to work with and where there is no conflict of interest. Reshma wants to use her knowledge and experience of direct payments and working with people with a learning disability. She is concerned not to be linked to an agency where she is known as a service user, as this might create difficulties in terms of power issues. The seeds of partnership are sown here and enable a conversation about the agency and the student that Reshma will work with.

Advocacy In Action learn from the start that it is important to set out the process of working together, both within the group and within the spaces it creates with other partners:

> ...our working agreements tend to be very simple and to centre on the commitment to learn with and from one another, to be willing to — and embracing of — challenge, to support each other and try not to hurt or offend, to be open to and welcoming of all that each person brings as a human being and as a partner, and at all times to be hopeful and positive of what can be jointly achieved.

For EMAPP, convening quite large meetings of different local authorities, service-user representatives and university staff, the focus is on how to manage the meetings so everyone is able to give their views and joint decisions can be reached. Larissa Barker expresses what she thinks is important in practical terms:

> Terms of reference are very useful to clarify roles and responsibilities — basics such as chairing arrangements, minutes taking, and attendance expectations. Good chairing ensures that everyone is heard and involved. An agenda helps participants know what is going to be discussed.

If meetings are to be truly inclusive, then the way that the meeting is run has to be understandable to everyone in it. EMAPP takes time to ensure that everyone sees minutes before the meeting and that anyone who does not find the written format or the language accessible has the minutes explained to them beforehand, as well as any written documents to be discussed during the course of the meeting.

It takes time to get it right for everyone. Professionals and academics are used to working in a way that assumes formal knowledge, understanding of language and communication through writing. Different sorts of knowledge and understanding and different ways of communicating can be unplanned for, uncomfortable, unwelcome, even threatening.

An assumption that only some in the group have 'special needs' which must be written down and somehow accommodated is quickly squashed as the service-user members point out early on in the meetings that *everyone* present has their personal and individual needs in learning how to work together.

It proves a real challenge to be inclusive, but the rewards for all members are great. Impersonal meetings filled with individuals who may not know each other very well can become liberating spaces where self-expression is modelled and encouraged. Partnerships will release these permissions if everyone is allowed to be themselves, rather than some being expected to 'fit in' to the conventions of others.

Advocacy In Action gives two examples of learning from early meetings with service providers. Polly recalls, as a lone service user in 1990, attending a joint planning group where no one shares their names with her or explains what is going on:

> I feel myself getting smaller and smaller – I sit here week on week and listen to all their long words, until I feel so small I feel invisible. And then I get fed up and angry. I stand up and I shout – 'Look! I'm here – Polly! I don't understand what you lot are saying – and I want you to tell me what that big jargon word you just said means!' Well! There's this big hush and everyone's looking at me – so I sit down and feel a bit embarrassed – and then this director woman looks me straight in the eye and says 'Thank you Polly, I didn't understand that word either, but I didn't have the guts to say so!'

Kevin Chettle has a meeting with a service director in 1992 to plan some Advocacy In Action training. He feels uncomfortable that the man sits behind a large desk with his files and folders. Kevin remembers a time when his life was kept in folders and filing cabinets by the people who ran the hospital where he lived. He feels put down that the information at this meeting is all in writing and feels separated by the desk and the power it represents. This new partnership does not make him feel welcome or involved, until Kevin invites the director to come round and sit next to him. Whereupon, the director jumps over his desk... 'Free at last!' he says, with a beaming smile!

For Stephen, working with people who lack capacity to make their own decisions, is about a person-centred approach. Sometimes it is possible to discuss the best way to work together with the person and their family, but sometimes this is more difficult. What is important here is that every effort is made to work with the person in a way that is the most reassuring for them:

> In some circumstances it is difficult to have agreement about how to work together. There are, though, several steps that might be taken to enable and encourage the person to participate as fully as possible in the decision-making process and in any action taken as a result of the decision. An example this may be choosing and adapting a location where people are more likely to feel at ease. Circumstances around the location can help to make communication easier. For example, if the room is too hot or too cold, or if there is lots of noise it might be distracting. In some cases the timing of the assessment too is very important. Some people function better in the evening, while others are better in the morning. In some circumstances the assessor might have to go backwards and forwards to suit the person's needs. Where possible, it might be important to delay the interview, particularly if this is likely to improve the overall outcomes. In all cases you don't want to rush the conversation but always allow enough time for conversations to take place and develop. In other circumstances you may need to take into account the person's state of mind and consider such things as the use of medication that may suppress a person and impact upon their ability to express themselves.
>
> It might be appropriate to sometimes engage support from someone acting as an advocate or even interpreter during the meeting. Complicated decisions, such as assessing where someone should reside in order to ensure that they receive necessary care and treatment, can throw up questions that are difficult to answer. Such questions need to be contextualised and broken down in order to be communicated effectively. We should think about methods of communication. Use simple language and break down the information into easy-to-understand points. Ask other people what is the best way of communicating and if necessary use specialist interpreters or signers to communicate with the person. Clearly getting things right at the start of the process requires planning and the gathering of background information is vital. By doing so the needs of the person are more likely to be met and a more meaningful partnership can be created.

Communication is vital from the outset to ensure that everyone involved in *React* understands the purpose of the partnership and what they are hoping to achieve:

> The time spent before work starts with the children sets the tone of the whole project and allows children to decide whether they want to be a part of it or not. The aim of this project is to promote a better understanding and foster better relationships between disabled and non-disabled children. It is time well invested and shows the children that their opinions are valued and their concerns listened to.

Good communication between staff at Beaufort and Colebourne Primary Schools before the partnership started is vital to its success. Teachers and support staff at Colebourne Primary are spoken to in order to find pupils whom they think might benefit most from the project. These selections strongly reflect the aim to promote equality and positive relationships between all pupils and staff in the schools. Once pupils from Colebourne are selected, they are spoken to about how they feel about pupils from Beaufort School and, most importantly, discuss whether or not they would like to take part in the partnership. It feels extremely important to promote an honest and open forum for the children to express their opinions.

Time is spent answering any questions the pupils from Colebourne have about their peers from Beaufort and to tackle any misconceptions through active discussion, rather than simply telling them they are 'wrong' and jeopardising the feeling of 'openness and honesty'.

PAct recognises that partnership can be a learning journey for everyone. Reflecting back on early principles, and how well they are upheld, helps to give some useful measure of where partnership succeeds and of where it falls down. Some academic partners acknowledge that:

> …working in the group is for us a challenging and interesting process. We are committed to a working partnership and the group agree to a good set of principles, but there seem to be few existing guidelines on how to actually *do it!*

The OPPS older people have a limited initial understanding of community research, of what their involvement might entail, and of what this could mean for them. A considerable amount of time, therefore, is devoted both to explaining the 'meaning' of research and to building up *ways of working together* so that people feel confident to engage with one another and to create spaces where they can use their own life experience to explore, challenge, build on and enrich conventional understandings of research.

The OPPS practical checklist asks if anyone needs:

Someone to sit at their side, a personal supporter, interpreter or signer? Picture or tape information, help with explanations, help with reading or writing? Help with refreshments, help to share an opinion, help to join in and feel part of things?

And it reminds people to try to:

...use simple language and give explanations − *ask* questions, *ask* for explanations. Say when we don't know or don't understand, say when we agree or don't agree. Always say 'well done' and mean it. Say sorry if we need to, it's a sign of strength. Try to be honest and open. Be friendly and supportive. Have fun!

In summary

EMAPP service-user members resist the attempt to redefine their involvement as 'special' and therefore different in some way, while Polly from Advocacy In Action describes for us the sense of isolation and frustration when she is met by a language that excludes her. Meanwhile, Kevin, from Advocacy In Action, celebrates getting a director to meet him on common ground.

It is important that some vision and values are shared by all at the very beginning of partnership. When this happens, it is then possible to agree roles and responsibilities, or at the very least, a common path to tread, to decide how to manage meetings or simply to engage with one another and make sure everyone is part of the dialogue and decision-making.

SHARED VALUES

Everyone brings their own values along with them when they enter into partnership, but individual values are not always compatible.

Sean's oral cancer makes it difficult for others to understand his views and feelings but Julie is able to interpret and act as advocate to ensure that his voice remains heard, respected and central from the start in determining the partnership pathway. Sean's key value is 'This is me – I'll never change – I don't want to change!' And the underlying message to partners is, 'So don't try to change me – even if I'm dying!' Rambler and roustabout Sean remains at heart the 'working-man-tramp' of his stronger days. He has no intention of going out passively, healthily or obediently.

This challenges those that would clean up his dying, that would remove the fags, the cans and the bottles, and remove Sean himself to the sorts of spaces which dying people are expected to inhabit. Such disparity in values is hard to accept within a partnership wholly dedicated to Sean's welfare. It prompts difficult questions on the very nature of 'well-being' and 'best interest', and real challenges as to whose interests and well-being are best being served. Whether a truly shared set of values is ever reached is questionable. But what is wholly evident is how willing some are to put aside their own strong values in order to respect and enable Sean's.

Shared values, however, are identified by many partnerships as a very important element in their successes, and have been cited above as part of the negotiation involved in setting up partnerships. Trish's experiences of partnerships develop first with other parents of children with disabilities and then with agencies and professionals. Her own values and the belief in the rights of all her family shape every partnership she works in. Trish recalls:

> ...at an early stage it feels like the relationship with statutory services is one where we are informed what we will be given as a family and it feels at this time that we have to fight for this. We have to find out what is 'out there' before we can access anything at all. It feels like without our research into what is available, we would not have the access to services, so the partnership doesn't feel at this stage to be equal. This is really demanding at a time when I feel I have to be strong for the whole family even though I am feeling vulnerable, scared for Emma's future and the future of our whole family. Through my research I discover many families with a disabled child have fragmented as a result of the huge pressures that such uncertainties placed on them. I desperately don't want that to happen to my family. I realise that if we are going through this, then other people will be as well. The belief in my family and my unshakeable belief that Emma is a person in her own right and not just a 'label' are my core values. From these core values, I want to

reach out to other parents/carers who share these core values. I look at what support groups are available at that time and I don't feel that they could give me what I need. I am introduced to three other families in similar situations by a professional. We are given a place to meet by the professional and we begin to meet once a month.

Advocacy In Action, in common with APTCOO, has been values-centred since its inception, and many core principles are embodied in those working practices previously described. Members reflect that:

As a group, we believe in the truth of our rich individual and collective experience. Advocacy In Action members come from many walks of life, usually treading the outer stony paths, because of our inside knowledge of poverty and denial. Within the Advocacy In Action partnership, disabled people, rough sleepers, substance users, transient and travelling people, survivors of care systems and people approaching the end of their lives unite with a belief in one another as people worthy of respect and love – partners with potential. Another value we share is the right to stick up for ourselves and for one another and we therefore reclaim the label 'challenging behaviour' to wear as a badge of pride. One other important value is the importance of learning and reflection and we apply this to all our alliances – within Advocacy In Action itself, and between our group and other partners.

Very simply, The Long Distance Gang agree:

To respect one another, to value everyone's contribution, to keep on trying to do our best, not to be too hard on ourselves if we get it wrong, to stay positive and to believe that hopes and dreams can come true.

June comments on her experience of working with different educational providers: 'There has been a steep learning curve, much to do with exploring the possible differences in value base, and some people are more open to doing this than others.' In order for meaningful dialogue to take place there need to be shared values founded on the principles and ethos expressed in the humanistic theory relating to unconditional positive regard. It is not always apparent that principles of respect and dignity are truly absorbed and adhered to in groups, resulting in a less than empathetic approach on the part of the power-holders. A lack of congruence between 'saying' and 'doing', or put another way, between the rhetoric and the reality, results in distrust between members of the group. Equally important is the need for respect of cultural difference when working in groups (culture in the widest sense of the word).

It is even more disappointing when there is an expectation that the values are understood and shared, although in the absence of shared values at the beginning, positive outcomes can still result when there is an eagerness to learn together. It is also sad to see the puzzlement and loss when groups 'fold' because of lack of attention at the beginning to the values underpinning the work of the group.

OPPS elders spend time agreeing a list of values that they want to try and work to. They need to relate them to their research task and to themselves as older people. Members decide that 'No one is *ever* "too old"! Anyone can be a researcher. There is nothing we cannot achieve if we believe in ourselves. Sharing power and purpose strengthens it. Together we *will* make things happen.'

In summary

A growing space is possible when partners have shared values, as this is a uniting factor. But June warns of tokenism and lip service to shared values at times, and of a shutting off to open discussion and exploration.

Sean's story shows that different values can and do collide and conflict. It suggests that service users have to be very strong to ensure their values remain at the centre within partnerships providing services to them – especially when such values are deemed 'irresponsible' or 'unsafe'. However, even when all partners do not hold the same values, it is still possible to create a growing space if people within the alliance are prepared to acknowledge difference and work together on a way forward.

POWER

The different partnerships have within them very different power dynamics, and it is a challenge to each partnership to address these.

For Reshma and Sherma, the power difference is immediately apparent as Sherma is assessing Reshma. Even within this unequal power relationship, a partnership emerges as each recognises the strengths within the other:

There is a power difference in this partnership but there is an implicit recognition of each other's strengths. We have a formal agreement of how we will work together and we are very business-like to start. We fall into a pattern of sharing things unconsciously.

Sherma unconsciously responds to Reshma's needs to keep it business-like at the beginning. This is also informed by Sherma's experience of practice, assessing where initial discussions about power issues are sometimes off-putting for students, as trust hasn't always been established at this point.

For Reshma, it is important to have some control over the initial meetings by keeping them quite formal. It is only when trust is established that they are freed up to actually talk about the power differences. With Sherma and Reshma, there are additional issues in relation to culture that further impact on the power relationship. Reshma is worried that, as Sherma shares her cultural background, she will be quite judgemental of her as a woman with a disability. Reshma has had these experiences in the past with other people from her culture. Reshma describes how, when she finds out Sherma's name and is told that she is going to assess her, she starts to worry. This is later acknowledged between them and is a means of learning for both of them, but initially it is a real barrier to open communication.

PAct members know of many troubled partnerships underlain by constraints or disparities – where *all* participants end up feeling floored and powerless at separate stages. But there is never sufficient time to discuss what is going on, nor perhaps the trust to open up and share. So these slippery issues lurk in the undergrowth as partners forge onwards against the clock.

The Asperger's Consultation Group feel that they are a 'partnership of equals'. For this group, the way it operates is to discuss all stages of the research they are doing together and agree a way forward together. There is a power difference between the group members and the researcher, but this is not felt by the group members. All group members consider that they have a valuable contribution to make and they know that they are listened to and perhaps more importantly, that their opinions are not just taken into account, but are acted on. No decisions about the research are made without discussion and agreement with all members, and so in this way the power is shared between the group.

Advocacy In Action recognises that words themselves are very powerful. Polly describes the early days:

We use words such as 'equal' and' normal'. We love these words and we want them so badly in our lives. This is because we've always been told we're not normal and that we got to do what other people tell us. We been told we've got limits. But when I take those labels off I feel that I can just grow and grow and nothing can stop me.

However, some years later Kevin says:

I don't say 'equal' because we don't all get treated the same − I say 'equal quality' because we are all human beings − human beings who get different treatment just because they are different people. I've learned it's okay to be different. I'm proud to say I'm disabled. But I expect the same opportunities as other people.

Advocacy In Action doesn't always live up to its own values. Members hold prejudices and air them, and the group invests huge effort and pain into addressing their inequalities. Learning to challenge and to be challenged hurts, and in the beginning there are many slammed doors and tears.

The older people of OPPS learn the power of challenge as they reflect on consulting with powerful council partners:

I'm sitting here thinking, 'Do people really want to listen to you?' Suddenly, people are listening, and wanting to join in, just joining in and I feel comfortable. I'm ready to go! I say to myself, 'They're here, here with us, here to listen and learn.'

…what will the reception will be − will we be labelled 'a group of old moaners'? No! They are taking us very seriously indeed!

…they are surprised. I watch their faces, everyone alert, listening, keenly listening − I am keenly surprised to pick up the feedback. They want more, more, more!

I can tell the audience are impressed, and I'm glad the councillors are taking it on board; it means a lot that they're willing to listen.

Listening to one another in the group, however, isn't something that everyone finds easy, in spite of the promises people have made to one another. Power in the OPPS group is contained at times within a small cluster of 'talkers', who forget to make space for others, in their enthusiasm to share experiences and memories. Reminiscences tumble all over one another as people fight to get a word in.

The older members of The Long Distance Gang look back to lives of rambling and freedom. Some wryly describe a care home existence as 'living in a prison' and 'serving life sentences'. They joke among themselves when they call the care staff 'warders' and 'keepers'. There is ambivalence between the security of feeling protected and cared for and the nostalgic longing for the openness of rough sleeping and tramping from town to town, and this yearning brings with it a sense of powerlessness, futility and a feeling of being trapped. So there are power differences between men who are residents and their care staff, and these impinge on wider partnerships within The Long Distance Gang. Discussions dry up quickly when staff invite themselves to those meetings held in one residential home. And a tension springs up for workers between what is a genuine interest in the group and a wariness of meeting one another within different boundaries and spaces.

There is a notion of 'territory being invaded' on many sides – The Long Distance Gang feels its freedom somewhat compromised, workers feel 'their' residents taken over by others and some report feeling 'left on the periphery'. But the motivation, focus and excitement of the older men are infectious and workers cannot help but begin to engage with the would-be travellers in a broader and more open way, with genuine interaction around shared experiences, and a growing sense of purpose and ambition.

The Long Distance Gang meetings create a positive space *apart from*, although sometimes *inside of*, the usual institutional confines and boundaries of care. Their chosen spaces are non-hierarchical, non-judgemental, non-therapeutic and not dependent on tasks or targets. Alcohol management in itself has no purpose or pressure within them.

Power differences *between* the members of the group are quite complex. The strategy of the older men to just 'switch off' when they feel like it denotes an anarchy that is in itself a flux of power and powerlessness. Using alcohol to dull the pain and problems puts men in control of what they do to their bodies and minds and yet at the same time takes control away.

And years later, as Sean's cancer spreads until he can hardly swallow his Guinness, he begins to shrink before our eyes, and weakness replaces strength. But as his illness progresses, there begins a most amazing reversal of power. Dave observes that 'As his health fails, Sean's personality and his life grow.' The *most frail* become the *most powerful*, when older residents also start to play a key role in supporting Sean's final months. And there is furthermore a good power flourishing among and between all his partners and a growing capacity among everyone to use their power to achieve Sean's wishes.

However, it is Sean himself who contributes to and indeed quite skilfully directs his pathway in a low-key yet confident manner. It is Sean who 'allows' friends, workers and other residents to find their place near him. And as he physically diminishes, it is Sean's inner power that blossoms and grows.

In summary

Power is found in unexpected places, both good and poorer varieties. PAct suggests that powerlessness is often a shared territory within partnerships, although infrequently acknowledged or discussed. OPPS demonstrates that 'powerless people' can and do disempower one another at times, while The Long Distance Gang shows that 'disinvolvement' can be a powerful strategy.

Power differences are a fact of life. In a growing space these still exist, but power can be named, owned and distributed and used positively to benefit all members of the partnership.

SUPPORT WITHIN PARTNERSHIPS

Partnerships can be a source of great support for those within them, both for the work that the partnership is involved in and also in terms of wider personal support.

This is very important for all Asperger's Consultation Group members. They say that 'people with Asperger's don't often get the opportunity to share how they feel.' And although the group is primarily set up to work on research together, they find it gives 'the chance to get feelings off your chest' and feel freed up to 'speak about experience without people trying to cure you.' This is really important and relates directly to the group members feeling they can be themselves. Members gain strength from one another. They feel understood and able to 'empathise with each other's experiences and feelings.' They also find that 'knowing each other's experiences makes us feel better.'

For Trish, the support comes from other families who share similar experiences. She recalls the growing partnership within the early days of APTCOO:

I meet with the other mothers and our children and we are able to share how we feel; our worries and concerns. We also celebrate the children and their accomplishments. As a group we are able to recognise what are real accomplishments for our children, which other people may not appreciate. We recognise how hard they have worked to do the things other children do easily, which they and their parents take for granted.

Advocacy In Action recognises that:

Our partnership does not operate between fixed office hours and we need to be available to one another at all times and in all facets of our lives. Partnership for us is not just a group activity but also a real life commitment.

Advocacy In Action are *there* for one another through thick and thin. As Brian Pendred describes: '…we just don't let one another go – we hang on in there and we do *not* let go!'

The colleague we support as we stand side by side in teaching situations may return to a restrictive care home, or end up in the cold to beg on the streets, find a fix, or sleep in the churchyard. They can be facing eviction or be on a downwards spiral to attempted suicide. They may face court or police bail. They might be terminally ill. It becomes impossible to work within 'part-time' partnerships when this is the reality of some of our members' lives.

Julie recalls standing alongside a pensioner colleague, backs against the door, as the landlord and his 'hard men' push for an illegal eviction. The week before, they stood in front of a class of students together. She also thinks about Lee, who has never missed a teaching date during her time in the group. Julie picks Lee up from the public toilets where she has spent the previous night. She has to come early in case Lee needs to 'score gear' before the class starts. Maureen is in tears again. They have changed the day on which her disabled daughter can visit. She tries to contain the heartbreak, as she assesses her students.

In situations like these, it becomes a natural extension of group activity to help one another survive what goes on outside. It is essential, however, that support offered is non-judgemental and can be taken or left without causing offence. Lee reflects that: '…this is the first group I have belonged to that hasn't been about "therapy" or making me "well". That's why I stick with it. It's opened things up for me in so many ways.'

Eileen O'Hara reserves the right to refuse help, insisting on her choice to ask for it when and only when she wants it. She knows her illness worries fellow members but reserves the dignity of directing her own support. Eileen knows, moreover, whom to turn to – and it is not always the people most 'able' to assist. Advocacy In Action has to think hard about this. What does it tells us about the power of a 'helper'? Partners need to ensure the role of 'supporter' is not restricted to or claimed by those identified as powerful or competent.

Support is dynamic throughout the time of Sean's journey to death, with everyone needing to give and to receive. Mutual support helps us take the risks associated with true liberation of wishes and possibilities, and later in accepting the impending loss of the central and much loved partner.

For Sean, the role of the older residents is pivotal in creating a shared space, where friends can be involved in his final months and ultimate death – there to drink him through the better days, to staunchly keep guard and provide a silent buttress when the going gets rough, and to howl with grief at the end. From the very outset, however, we all own an absolute naked vulnerability and reach out to one another in ways that leap across the boundaries separating familiar from unfamiliar, personal from professional, and the living from the dying.

Good support too is set up in OPPS between people who by virtue of older age are usually deemed as being on the receiving and 'needy' end. Clear support principles are established and set down, but over and above these is a natural empathy that enables older people to befriend and support one another in meetings and during intervals between. Older people say that their shared experience is a support in itself: '…just to realise you are not the only one who feels so lonely…'

Group members comfort one another and boost morale. Within the OPPS meetings, people compensate for one another's hearing loss, visual impairments and mobility needs, explain what is going on and sit next to newer members. It must be said, however, that the same level of support isn't made available to everybody, as we discuss later (see p.124).

There is a huge community of support operating in The Long Distance Gang among men with a shared experience of hardship, and between these men and the community volunteers. Residential care staff partners feel supported when they can latch on to meetings and by the understanding that The Long Distance Gang offers a great vehicle to be part of new ways of working that generate previously unsurpassed levels of response from everyone, whether they be residents, workers or volunteers. Care staff partners gain support from within the partnership, in learning how to create a 'culture of possibility and hope' rather than just *warehousing* and maintaining safe routines for people labelled as having complex pasts and limited futures.

It is validation of shared experience that unites the people of the Asperger's Consultation Group with Advocacy In Action members, with Trish's group of mothers, with the elders of OPPS, with the travellers to Ireland and with all who journey alongside Sean in his care home. Shared experience leads to strong supportive groups. It is more of a challenge to get such a shared sense and strength of support within partnerships where there are not necessarily such common bonds.

There can be lip service to support that isn't really there in more formalised groups. One danger of being used to committing principles to paper is that they remain there – as though their existence is an end in itself. For some, the 'partnership chatter' can become empty noise, and the louder the noise, the less certainty what lies beneath! It is thus communicated to Advocacy In Action by reflective practitioners that: '... using words like "partnership", "freedom" and "choice" serve precisely to disguise the fact that these do not exist.'

PAct members find that although partners invariably promise as a group to listen to one another, it does not always happen. And some voices get to be more 'valuable' than others, although this isn't a clear professional versus service-user split. Are some inevitably failed within the group process? And are some conversely deemed to require more support than they truly need?

For *React*, the support which the teachers give to the children in turn led to non-disabled children physically supporting their disabled peers, while disabled children in turn support the learning and value development of non-disabled colleagues:

> All of the sessions are interactive and child-led. The pupils from Colebourne Primary are able to support the pupils with learning difficulties from Beaufort in a number of ways. They enable them to make choices through showing preferences of music, props, colours

and movements. The pupils communicate their preferences through facial expression, returning to the same activity or item repeatedly or showing interest through eye contact or repeated exploration. The pupils from Colebourne also support their peers by copying their movements, enabling them to feel a greater sense of empowerment and control over the world around them. Pupils from Beaufort are able to show support to their peers from Colebourne by interacting with them and building friendships.

Such mutual support is not always realised, however, and June comments:

> 'Support' has to be worked at because of the power imbalance and differential. It is assumed always that it is only the service users who need support. In my experience, support for the other allies tends to be seen as learning/development. I wonder why that is?

PAct reflects how this ties in to that early service-user experience of EMAPP, where the meeting records their 'special needs' for joining in, in order to accommodate them in the group. EMAPP service-user members are quick to point out that *everyone* present has some needs in learning how to work together, and stipulates that an amendment to the 'written record' be made to reflect this. Service-user co-chair, Kevin Chettle, says he doesn't want to be seen as 'special' or different at meetings, but adds that he does want a fair chance to join in.

In summary

Advocacy In Action draws our attention to the power of being the 'support definers and support givers' and to the powerlessness of being on the receiving end at times. They point further to the reality that good support spills over the boundaries of formal partnership within office hours. Lee reflects that support on her own terms may not be focused on her 'condition' as perceived by others. Both Sean and OPPS testify to the strength and dignity of 'peer support'.

Advocacy In Action warns that the language of support within partnership does not necessarily herald its presence, and that language can indeed be the 'invisible shot' that dulls our understanding of this. PAct, meanwhile, warns against falsely assuming that people need high levels of support to join in, and asks, support for whose benefit? June extends this concept by showing how what is support for the layperson becomes 'capacity-building' for the professional. The reframing of support for those who are in less powerful or valued positions is not only unhelpful but reinforces unequal power relations.

In a growing space, members feel truly supported by each other. There is recognition that all within a partnership need the support of others. Shared experience can lead to support, but it can also grow from mutual understanding and acceptance. All people benefit from the support of one another regardless of position. This is celebrated within partnerships where members are all respected as people first.

TRUST

We have seen examples of where people have found support in their partnerships. This support comes from a trust of other group members. Reshma and Sherma talk about how their trust in each other has built up. They acknowledge that this is not automatic or immediate. Trust has to be earned. Reshma reflects:

> ...at this early stage my personal opinion is that this scenario is not a true partnership as we do not share the same risks and power. I have been in previous 'partnerships' where I felt used – as I was only invited because I was a black Asian lady using a wheelchair and this fact makes funding easier to apply for. Experiences like this have made *me* wary of developing trust too quickly and 'running before you can walk'. It is easier to take smaller steps towards creating trust – it is almost about testing each other out...

Sherma also has worries about entering into a partnership:

> ...it is more about feeling anxious not to be patronising and about recognising that we each have different expertise and not assuming that the 'assessment power' has to be exercised all the time. I bring with me wariness about not patronising Reshma. I am conscious that I need to step back and not take control in situations involving others. It is important not to let my anxieties get in Reshma's way and for me to recognise that Reshma is well able to manage these situations and would seek support when necessary. The support feature is here because I understand my role and I bring unconscious experience with me in terms of my style of working. When we get to sharing personal stuff, this changes, but it takes us a long time to get to this point.

For both Reshma and Sherma, the journey to trusting each other is intertwined with their ability to acknowledge issues of racism and culture. For Reshma, this is a risky discussion to have, as she has learned to her cost in the past. It isn't until Sherma shares her own experiences that Reshma feels secure enough in the relationship to have this discussion. Reshma recalls:

> I become aware that I haven't talked about my own values. I will need to be able to do this with a student. We have one session when Sherma talked about her experience of discrimination.

Reshma is doing other work that has made her think of discrimination and this learning leads to an agenda of discussion where the support begins to change. As Sherma shares her experiences of discrimination, Reshma begins to question her own experiences and starts to think about jokes and conversations that people in the past have made. Reshma begins to think about her own identity as a black, Asian, disabled woman: 'I have only thought about myself as a disabled person previously as that is where the biggest challenges have been for me.' Sherma recognises:

> I have had to address experiences of racial discrimination and I know that if Reshma hasn't faced up to her experiences of discrimination then it will be really difficult for her to support a student to understand discrimination... We begin to really know about each *other* at this point. After this point, Reshma begins to set the agenda.

For Reshma, this is a really important time in the relationship. It is when it becomes a partnership and when she feels equal and able to set the agenda.

Although people might assume that the ideal situation is to match two women from the same cultural background, for Reshma, this is a barrier. She has previous experience '...of Asian professionals, judging me in terms of cultural expectations. A particular Asian professional made it clear that I should stay living with my family rather than promote independence.' Reshma has developed her own identity and thinks that only white people can understand it. She sees relating to white people as a place of safety and so working with Sherma presents a risk to that safety and to the identity that she has developed.

Sherma's social work education gives her the opportunity to question her cultural values. Reshma has not previously had the opportunity to question cultural values. She assumes that Sherma will come with a particular set of cultural values. Sherma is able to help Reshma own and challenge these assumptions about her. It is Sherma's ability to share on a personal level that opens Reshma up.

There are also practical matters that help develop the trust to the point that Reshma is prepared to be open in talking about her identity with her assessor. Sherma is aware of her role in making 'reasonable adjustments', and tries to facilitate resource needs that Reshma identifies for herself. The specific example of this is the investigation with library services and publishing companies of the availability of electronic books – 'We were successful in getting an electronic copy of the key text from the publisher at no additional cost.' From this experience Reshma is able to go on to negotiate with other publishers access to copies of electronic books when purchasing books for her personal use. Sherma acknowledges: 'I feel I have to prove myself by these little actions.' Reshma also feels Sherma is proving herself by allocating sufficient time for supervision – that Sherma is really interested in developing her: 'I have had the experience of social workers and physios coming in to see me who always apply very strict time constraints...'

Stephen also recognises the need to take the necessary time. Trust in the context in which he works requires a commitment to get to know someone and what is important to the person. This is also vital to his assessment of what is in the person's 'best interest':

> There have been times when people have been happy in their beliefs and circumstances even though they are not fully aware of them. It is important to speak to them about what they are familiar with and it is good to talk to people about their lives and things that they are keen to speak about. This is important to build a relationship of trust. People who lack capacity are often happy in their own minds and are engaged at some level. You can't speak at them but with them. You use people's understanding of their context to build up trust...

Nes, film-maker on The Long Distance Gang journey, reflects on the dilemma of building trust in spaces where there is not necessarily a 'shared experience':

> ...do we all contribute our memories and experiences? The journey and film are rooted in the memories and experiences of certain people in the group but not all. I feel at times an 'outsider'. I question what I

bring. I can only bring my willingness to learn. Nothing is worse than entering into this space blindly and without respect, without attempting to understand, or even feeling the need to.

There is also a danger in which you can go another way – you begin to feel you are not worthy of entering a space which others have earned through their direct experience. And that can have as many problems and difficulties. You then risk fawning over people, condescending and patronising, believing you can't possibly understand.

Nes points us towards the danger of feeling pity or shock but without empathising – of becoming voyeuristic and consuming, watching, but unchanged, just guilty and more than a tiny bit relieved when we can excuse ourselves and make a hasty exit. This is what happens when we scan the outer story without looking too closely at and relating to the common lived understandings beneath. Nes is able to discover, in his personal life as a younger English man, those shared themes and feelings – powerlessness, resilience, survival, capacity, loss – that helps him make the empathic bridge between his own story and those of the older Irish drinkers.

Advocacy In Action confirms an essential collective belief in the group and explains how this trust nurtures and heals people after all their difficulties and atrocities experienced:

> Brian remembers years of abuse in the care home where he went to be 'looked after'... Kevin recalls how he and Jonathan were tortured and forgotten, in a cruel hospital. Members reflect that they have turned to one another as a community of survival and they place their fullest trust in this community.

Advocacy In Action recognises that 'wanting to trust' is very important to members, within both the earlier and the more recent partnerships.

Kevin unconditionally forgives those people who hurt him, when he says '...everyone is an equal quality human being – we love to give everyone chances.' It is a deeply moving statement, particularly considering the huge betrayals and hurts inflicted by some people onto others, too often in the name of formal care. Perhaps it is something to do with the collective nature of Advocacy In Action's earliest members, many of whom are learning disabled. Pushing aside all mythologies about people with learning disabilities, Advocacy In Action recognises in them an innate willingness to trust and an ability to operate from heart level. Non-learning-disabled partners learn from and embrace this openness into a richer way of being. They in turn provide the protective layer to safeguard trust from being shredded. It is a symbiosis of heart, savvy and mind.

This partnership between *heartwise, headwise* and *streetwise* in Advocacy In Action enables trust to blossom and thrive within the group and within all the alliances it builds outside.

In mapping out the course of Sean Travers' cancer and its terminal prognosis, Sean, Julie, Nes, Dave and allies fully recognise the importance of *self-belief* when discovering new pathways together. Sean completely trusts in the life he is creating in his final months. His fellow explorers find in themselves a trust to achieve it with him. From roots of self-belief, we reach out to, and begin to depend on, one another. Our *inner trust* helps us to take the risks of trusting each other. Inner trust is perhaps less about complacency and security and more about *an utter willingness to be opened up and unsure.*

Sean's final months illuminate for us that it is not necessarily the cosy, predictable partnerships that signify success. Good spaces do not always feel comfortable, or indeed safe. So in talking about *trust* it becomes very important to distinguish it from the easy and empty 'taking things for granted' that sprawls all over the surface of less-genuine partnerships, and smothers those truly brave places where beliefs, ideas and action embed themselves.

Can real trust exist within formal partnerships of professionals and service users and carers? As a member of PAct, Julie reflects:

> ...the starting point has to be our shared task-based purpose. There will always be a tension between getting the job done and how we meet as humans.
>
> In some ways, as a service user, I feel I'm on professional soil by permission rather than right. That's not to say I feel unwanted — far from it! There is a welcome here from some partners, if not all — a welcome to and a wanting for the ideas of partnerships. But it does not always feel to me like a truly shared space, where we can all be free to be ourselves. Let me try to explain. I question how often within these professional settings we are able to make honest exchanges of personal experience. I know that we who use services are deemed 'experts by experience'. We bring experience to compliment others' 'expertise'. I think this acceptable, until I start to consider where in all of this is *my*

expertise and *their* experience? I find my professional partners often closed to talking about themselves or their lives in any open way unless related to the nine-to-five contexts of their work and the job in hand. Am I being unfair here?

An academic partner makes an important response to Julie:

...wider trust *can* be difficult — you don't necessarily want your own colleagues who you see every day to know some things — you have to be able to choose who you feel *safe* to discuss private issues with — a key boundary in any group.

In EMAPP, trust within the group — or at least in the core of the group — develops through working with shared responsibility for important tasks. Again this trust is earned through service users demonstrating capacity. It might not always have been so embedded at the beginning. Once more, however, the forum's *willingness* to expose itself to co-working and co-production is there from the start.

This enables group outputs, presentations and submissions that are fully collaborative. Julie considers the benefits of this:

I feel proud to see our names alongside academic and professional colleagues, as a right, rather than a concession or a tick-box requirement.

Julie knows trust within the EMAPP core group has strengthened through tackling difficulties together. She recalls a personally testing experience where she resorts to challenge, asking colleagues to let go of personal boundaries and to give her some 'real' support. The honest dialogue, around what can and cannot be between them, nurtured trust.

Jackie also reflects on her experience of working in EMAPP:

Coming from social work at a time when the value of service users and carers working alongside professionals to shape services was in its infancy (at least in practice), I was not used to involving them in every stage of my work. But as the programme leader for the post-qualifying award for social work with adults there is a requirement that I do just this. I begin with willingness but also much trepidation as I have always been very clear where the boundaries lay between myself and those whom I had previously assessed and supported. This new way of working is a real challenge. How do you do this? How do you involve service users and carers in every aspect of your work, as well as six local authorities and a private sector agency and still ensure that all the various professional and academic requirements are met? There is a new expectation that I will be open and share as a person as well as presenting my professional persona (which has been finely honed over the years).

Well, the answer I have found is to be open and honest about what needs to be done and why and what the requirements are. Then people, be they service users, carers or other professionals, will respond to this and help rather than hinder. I am a born worrier (so my children tell me) and I like to make sure that everything works and I make myself responsible for this. I absolutely am accountable for what happens on the programme, but I have learned that I can trust others to help me with this.

The requirement to involve others, both professional and service users and carers, started out as something I knew I had to do and had to learn how to do – what I hadn't expected were the riches that this partnership would bring, not only in terms of having a good programme, but personally. Being in the EMAPP space has brought me the gift of friendship, loyalty and a shared vision – this can't happen without a great deal of trust.

Mark Lymbery, Associate Professor of Social Work at the University of Nottingham, reflecting on his very long-term relationship with Advocacy In Action, highlights the importance of trust, and of investing the necessary time in building it up:

> ...in any aspect of life and work, the more people work together, the more likely it is that trust and confidence will develop. Without trust it is unlikely that an amicable and supportive relationship would still exist. It is therefore not possible to develop patterns of effective joint working in a short timescale.

Mark looks back over 20 years of shared experience with Advocacy In Action, from developing complaints procedures and the revised Diploma in Social Work in the early 1990s and his appointment in 1995 at the University of Nottingham, which, through partnership with Advocacy In Action, is by then well ahead of its time in forging ahead with service-user engagement: '...this sense of history is important in understanding where we are now. Any successes we have been able to achieve are the product of a lot of joint working.'

OPPS also has trust between its core members, although not necessarily extended to newer faces unless they are judged to 'fit'.

There is, nevertheless, an unquestioning trust of professional partners, based on a gratitude for their presence and acceptance of their motives and values. This is not shared by all, however! Julie and Reshma both recognise huge power differences within the partnership. In her relatively powerful position as independent consultant, Julie feels able enter into some confrontation with local authority partners to preserve a degree of balance and equity. Reshma, however, recognises her own specific personal vulnerability:

> I am not sure whether we could have pulled this off without the knowledge, skills and dynamic persona of Julie Gosling. It must be recognised that she had challenging moments with Leicester City Council behind the scenes. As a person who uses services indirectly provided by the local authority, I do not feel that I would have been able to hold my stance during any tensions, for fear of losing services. I feel I have to say this because the comments from the interviews endorse that there will always be power differences when working with people who use services. The council must recognise and own this.

Reshma's experience in OPPS points to the importance of honesty in acknowledging power differences within partnerships. While power differences in themselves can act against trust, their honest exposure can promote it. The ability and willingness to challenge can also be a good indicator of trust within any relationship.

In summary

Trust is not cheap currency. Reshma recalls losing trust where she has felt in the past to have been exploited, devalued or misjudged on racial and cultural grounds. Nes, on the other hand, recognises that he enters The Long Distance Gang space carefully with eyes and heart wide open and a willingness to learn. Nes, like Sherma, worries about being seen as patronising. Nes also warns us against the danger of 'voyeurism' in partnerships – of interacting without engaging or empathising.

Sean's story unpicks trust as a willingness to be tested and laid bare to uncertainty and risk. PAct draws attention to the limits to wider trust within more formal partnerships. Meanwhile, EMAPP returns to the necessity of trust being earned through investments of effort and time.

Trust results from the efforts made to understand others in a partnership and to be prepared in turn to be understood. In a growing space, different levels of trust might exist between members, but trust has to exist as a baseline in the ability of others to work together within the context of the alliance.

CHALLENGING EACH OTHER IN A PARTNERSHIP

This is a difficult area as challenging people can lead to disharmony in a partnership, so sometimes people choose not to do so. However, in any partnership it should be possible to challenge others within it and be enriched rather than impoverished by the experience.

React is set up partly to challenge the values of some of the children in the school who had not previously had the opportunity to think of disabled fellow pupils in a different way. The task here is to challenge values in a way that respects all of the children:

> We tackle negative views or misconceptions by positive reinforcement. We want the children to work together in positive ways which alter their opinions and help them to feel empowered, rather than telling them how they should think and what they should believe.

For June it is important to challenge 'robustly but in a constructive, open and honest way.' As a service user, June feels when she needs to challenge professionals that they often 'draw back from doing the same in a mistaken belief that they are being sensitive to the needs of service users.' June believes that it is important to be sensitive, but that all group members should be open to challenge as long as it is done in a respectful way. In her experience, if relationships develop within the partnership, then this becomes less of an issue, and people are more open to challenge each other.

Ed and Sarah have learned to challenge, by getting to know one another well and recognising when the necessity arises. They go on to discuss whatever the issue is. They both feel able to challenge and, moreover, to invite challenge from one another: 'By questioning why we have done things and creating space for this to happen – we recognise each other's non-verbal cues.' Sarah might say 'Ed, what is in your head?', giving Ed the opportunity to say something if he wants. Ed often says 'Are you are alright?', which serves as a cue for Sarah to respond.

Conflict arises initially between Reshma and Sherma around their understanding of racism and identity. Their relationship grows as Reshma realises that Sherma's role is 'to assess, not to judge': 'We challenge one another through the discussions of identity. Reshma has internalised discrimination and put it 'at the bottom of her stomach.'

The same issues can be seen at work in this partnership – it is through getting to know each other and through a growing trust that Reshma and Sherma become able to share experiences and then understand them in a way that Reshma has shied away from before.

The issue of conflict and disagreement is never too far away for Stephen, as in his job he has to make decisions on behalf of people that they may not be happy with:

> Often there comes a point when we have to raise difficult issues with the person. For example, where is the person going to live? The person being assessed might believe they are able to live independently and without risk when you believe something very different. In these circumstances we may have to raise the difficult issues and challenge their reality. This is particularly true when people have lived a certain lifestyle which might have included a degree of risk-taking above that that is 'ordinarily' expected. This makes the principle of trust even more important as the person must feel able to add their perspective on their ability so that the best outcome can be achieved.

Stephen is very aware of the power that he has, and for him, this makes his task of understanding the person all the more important:

> …the person's past and present wishes, their beliefs, values, previous life choices and their abilities in the current context must be considered. Although the circumstances of this type of decision-making are quite different from other examples of partnerships we are exploring, they have a number of things in common. For example, it highlights the importance of anti-discriminatory practice and being non-judgemental. People who lack capacity should be treated equally and with respect, and we should certainly not fall into the trap of making judgements on the basis of a person's age, appearance, disability or their behaviour.

Stephen welcomes being challenged about his assessments by the person he is assessing as well as by the person's family. He is always prepared to re-examine what he has thought to ensure that he has assessed accurately. Here, the values of the assessor are of such vital importance. The assessor has to reflect constantly on their assessments to make sure they are truly in the 'best interests' of the person.

Advocacy In Action now reclaims the label 'challenging behaviour' as a flag for rights-based work. But back in the early 1990s, challenge is a new and sometimes hard experience:

> We have to support each other to learn how to challenge, how to receive challenge, and how to see challenge as healthy and positive. But why is challenge so difficult?
>
> As Polly says: 'I didn't have a voice and I didn't have any words because "that lot" [professionals] took 'em all off me – but they're *my* words now – so please listen to me!'
>
> It is such a small, fragile and easily bruised confidence at the start – it is hard work to begin to believe in the new rights and freedoms we are giving to ourselves – such as having a voice, making choices, being listened to and respected, let alone being able to exercise them. No wonder that challenging one another feels so very, very unsafe! We all take challenge very personally to heart, as criticism and rejection. We have to learn to separate the behaviour from the person to try to make challenge bearable. Welcoming inner challenge as the friend of change is difficult and uncomfortable.
>
> Meanwhile, of course, we are loud and vociferous in our outside challenges towards 'that lot'! Looking back, it is the rawness of this anger and an unrestrained energy to challenge that drives those first days. Although challenge becomes better tempered and regulated as time goes by – and perhaps more effective – we can't help but look back to the early battles with a nostalgia that mourns something lost and irretrievable but deeply treasured. We must never, never become too cosy in our partnerships!

Challenging *one another*, however, is something to be maintained from the start within Advocacy In Action. Some powerless people have this inclination to put others down as inferior, in order to feel better about themselves. Others know this is not on, when they hear their unkind remarks:

> …at least we're not 'mental' or 'wheelchairs' or 'special needs'.

> …some of the awful comments people make, to try and feel superior or secure! And that's before we get stuck in the thorns of ethnicity, gender, sexual preference.

One big problem is that the differences in levels of understanding and capacity to understand within the group make talking about 'oppression' in any inclusive way a difficult challenge. Another problem is the poverty of many people's experience and their lack of opportunity to ever consider human difference as a positive. The sterile institutional systems, where people have been and continue to be kept, do not often give cause to celebrate. Their blinkeredness and bad power are poisoned soil for harvesting the wealth of diversity and human potential.

> So we have to learn to accept and welcome difference in ourselves and others, to challenge on behalf of others and ourselves, and to be challenged back in return, as individuals and as a group. And this is by no means easy.

OPPS members too initially find challenge and accepting challenge extremely difficult. There are first the generational notions of 'courtesy', 'respecting professionals' and 'knowing your place'. Further, a lack of confidence and the erosion of self-image accompanying the invisibility of older age, particularly after retirement or poor health, lead previously assertive people, including one-time activists and campaigners, to feel extremely wary about speaking out. Although there are pensioners involved in local community protest and politics who can really hold their own, there are not nearly enough!

Within OPPS, learning to accept challenge is difficult. One member leaves OPPS when she cannot come to terms with it. Challenges from people seen as 'important' meet with a different response to peer challenge. While the latter is received with heated debate, the former is usually acquiesced to − on the surface at least − often with apologetic telephone calls to ensure that members have not fallen from grace! The group need to get themselves to a point where they can confidently challenge professional allies rather than hang onto every word with something approaching reverence, accompanied by repeated gratitude for 'taking the time to talk to us', 'letting us respond', 'enabling our group to continue!'

The OPPS launch nevertheless provides a wonderful opportunity for members to speak out and throw their gauntlet to provider partners. Older people find a confidence in their solidarity, which, backed up by strong event planning and facilitation, enables them to speak eloquently and with passion to service heads and care managers. The older presenters are overwhelmed with the impact they made and much empowered by it.

It is very difficult at times for The Long Distance Gang partners to challenge one another in ways that don't seem patronising or aggressive. Strategies of hedging round, trying to reason with, or adopting a superior 'expert stance' have little effect. The best challenges come from an older Irish woman volunteer who gives as good as she gets, swears outrageously and threatens to put manners on everyone if they don't 'shift straight back into gear and get on with the work!' This 'in your face challenge' travels with the group to Ireland and proves useful in different ways and settings. Rough banter becomes the vehicle for challenge, albeit with a vernacular that might raise an outsider's eyebrow. But shouting across the room to 'Shut up and listen, you old Cavan donkey!' earns far more respect and attention than a gentler 'Let's just sit down and talk about things'! The language that hacks out routes travelled together finds these coarsest paths to map out and test the partnership. But who says that challenge is a smooth or easy ride?

And it is challenge that keeps us alive at raw points along Sean Travers' illness in 2010. We have to chivvy one another to keep on going when pain, worry and exhaustion take over. Sean is often the one to confront his partners, threatening to walk out or hit out in retaliation for things not going his way. The only means to resolve this at times is to pitch headlong into battle. Yet within each confrontation is the knowledge that we are all fighting the same enemy.

There are huge challenges for the care staff to 'let go' and take the risks associated, say, with relinquishing the controlled drug register to 'volunteers', as Sean plans to travel back once more with friends of his choice to say a last farewell to family and birth village in Ireland, eight weeks before his death. This is not at all straightforward from the staff's point of view. Dave Milburn owns that there are those who feel the journey could hasten Sean's demise and there are accusations of 'all too ambitious!'

But these fears find a perspective, when Dave challenges and motivates his team to see the bigger picture – of entrusting Julie, Sean and Nes '…to get on with things in a way that they themselves are wholly comfortable with.'

Everything is still risk assessed, nevertheless, in accordance with rigid dictates from 'above', and Dave, with his team at '32', use their evaluations to help them take a firm stand against higher management, who are questioning on what authority '32' *dares* to release a dying resident to the hands of 'untrained volunteers'. In the final count, Sean, Nes, Julie, Dave and the rest of the team wholly believe in one another and in the challenges they have set themselves. Everyone agrees that the journey will go ahead.

Julie reflects on how a less well-rooted partnership may be squashed by the challenge of risk, and on how potentially damaging this could be:

> ...sometimes, the risk seems to weigh the partnership down and crush it — but we damage the very core of our well-being — our emotional and spiritual wholeness — if we deny people life-breathing opportunities in the final stages of their dying — and fail to support them to face and live the risks involved. Risk-averse living just makes people wither up from the inside.

Within more formal partnerships, different ways of working, engaging with and challenging one another can generate discomfort. While professionals challenge through the language of policy and technical speak, service users and community activists may feel more at home with a 'say it as it is'. David meets Goliath when a PAct service-user member with relatively little experience or confidence in sticking up for herself openly challenges a powerful partner's practice.

In all good partnerships there are bound to be differences of opinions and conflicts. The key path many partnerships take to deal with this is through having relationships where people are heard, understood and valued. Even if agreement does not seem possible, it is the *way* people treat one another within the process of exploring solutions that is so important.

In summary

React shows how positive engagement can result in young people challenging their assumptions of one another. June points to the importance of partners being open to respectful challenge and Sarah and Ed demonstrate how this works for them in practice. Reshma and Sherma hail challenge as the promoter of growth, and Stephen welcomes it as the enabler of good practice.

Both Advocacy In Action and OPPS have had to learn to challenge and be challenged and find the confidence and the courage to embrace it as a positive. Meanwhile, The Long Distance Gang and Sean's partnerships embody challenge as a way of mutually respecting, motivating and moving forward.

A growing space is not a place where nobody challenges. It is a space where people contest respectfully, and where challenge is seen as an opportunity to reflect, improve and understand self and others better.

Chapter 2

SOWING THE SEEDS

LEARNING FROM EACH OTHER

One of the joys and riches of being in a partnership, apart from the support that it can provide, is the vast amount that people can learn from one another.

The *React* partnership (see p.30) facilitates disabled and non-disabled children working together to create a performance:

> This project gives our pupils the opportunity to have a greater impact on the world around them and develop awareness. With the smallest movement, they are able to influence light, colour and sound, which encouraged them to build concentration, visual tracking and cause-and-effect skills. Pupils were able to steer the learning in their preferred direction and build skills through their own exploration of movement, sounds and visual stimuli. They were able to react to the cause-and-effect nature of the art work and solve problems by repeating an action which had a favoured effect. The pupils from both schools are able to learn from one another by working collaboratively as equal partners and by exploring their own likes and interests as well as acknowledging each other's.

Much is learned by all the pupils about how to perform using technology and movement, but more significantly, the children learn to value each other and have the opportunity to grow to like one another.

Learning about the law ensures that when other parties deem Sean Travers Lynch's more risky choices as 'unwise' (see p.25 for more on 'My Final Journey'), Sean and his partners can point to his legal right to decide.

Partners learn something very important about the politics of the term 'well-being'.

> This has different meanings for different people, and that rather than person-centring, it can shift the focus to the interests of organisations, practitioners and service providers. We also learn that 'safeguarding' at its very best is as much about the management of possibility as a hindrance of harm. We learn to see the *opportunity within the risk*.

Partners learn more about controlled medication, both its legal requirements and about the dignity of self-regulating. Volunteers, friends, older residents, care staff, manager advocates and, of course, Sean himself, all contribute to deeper shared understandings – dedicated but different people learning with and from one another.

Dave Milburn reflects how the learning is enabled and directed by Sean himself:

> ...he endures great pain at times, which is humbling and affecting, but inspirational. Sean 'allows' staff and residents to find their place in the process. Occasionally this is about us all learning how to find some balance between medication and alcohol.

Volunteers and residents learn about the 'bigger picture' of how staff are often constrained and limited by their formal roles. They are also able to gain useful knowledge by engaging as partners in professional skills and procedures. Practitioners, in turn, draw from the lived experiences of their service users and from the innovative daring solutions of ordinary people dealing with extraordinary things. Swept along this intense learning curve, mutual experience, insight and appreciation firmly bind people together.

Back in time, to the planning for Ireland, and Long Distance Gang members are starting to work as a team! Partners learn to value their own and other's strengths, while remaining honest about personal needs. Removing assumptions around who can do what is essential. So, for example, when the minibus is discussed, the age, capacity and alcohol needs of some members do not preclude their involvement in planning who will drive and maintain the vehicle. Shared experience of years of driving (with or without a licence!) are thrown into the pot and learned from.

Everyone's contribution is truly invaluable and helps make collective decisions that delegate responsibility to each individual for some part of the whole task. The group recognises that everyone's skills are needed, that discrete chores can be split up and shared, and that the best learning embraces many different experiences.

Advocacy In Action focuses on positives – what people *can* do, and not what they can't. As Kevin Chettle recalls 'I'm always being told about my special needs – never about my special *strengths*.' Advocacy In Action partners encourage pride in achievement and also sharing. People learn that sharing skills improves and expands them. For example, partners help one another learn all the bus routes from the day centre to the advocacy office. Members who can read put information onto tapes for their colleagues, who in turn support others to learn to interview and research. Friends interpret one another's signs and sounds and then build joint presentations. When one member gains a skill or learns something useful, they spread it around the group. Every new skill is welcomed, passed on and shared. Personal qualities also – for example, Christine's kindness, Jonathan's openness – are praised and duplicated as people celebrate and learn from the best in one another.

PAct (Our Promise to Act) (see p.29) members contribute both academic and life experience to shared processes. But a tutor within one such partnership reflects to PAct that it doesn't always produce the ideal 'product' if too much time is spent on the *way* people work together rather than on *what* they produce:

> ...when good work is produced, it is because the *context* is fully understood. Understanding of the social work context and user perspective context can be missing from either service users or people without experience of service use.

PAct members, however, feel that group dynamics and internal and external power factors can dampen or inhibit challenge and stifle people learning about one another in any positive way. This is now starting to make some individuals feel compromised within their partnerships.

Gina Hardesty, on behalf of PAct, summarises the conflict between wanting and needing to challenge but being constrained or suppressed within formal partnerships. She admits to wanting to get out of the statutory partnership game: 'I want to go back to the outside in order to have more freedom and to speak the truth'. Julie also experiences a conflict between not wanting to abandon professional allies while knowing she, too, is far more effective from the outside:

> ...the community and service-user collaborations I engage within are dynamic and usually based on vibrant relationships full of shared passion and commitment. These are the active spaces where I feel true growth and learning taking place for me and my partners.

For the East Midlands Adults PQ Partnership (EMAPP) (see p.21), nevertheless, the learning from one another is a genuine and enduring strength. Each individual brings with them a different perspective and a wealth of experience, as academic or practitioner or user of services. Working with service-user partners who are fully involved in all aspects of developing and teaching the PQ programme proves to be a great opportunity to learn how to work differently. However, in order for this learning to take place, people have to be prepared to listen to what is being said by others and to give the opinions respect. This requires humility on the part of all to make this partnership work. For those who are 'professionals', this means sharing power in meetings and acknowledging the power of lived experience.

For service-user colleagues it entails a willingness to dovetail radical views into professional agendas, an occasional acceptance of compromise, and a commitment to take on shared responsibility within formal academic processes and programmes. There is plentiful opportunity to gather other different and wider perspectives in regard to current 'on the ground' problems and solutions within service provisions. Last, but not least, service users as 'opportunists' grab the chance to increase their knowledge, as educators, truth-seekers and scholars in their own right.

Jackie, the programme leader, finds such learning of immeasurable value. She recognises the real strength of working with others in this manner and understands that while not everything goes smoothly, she is being challenged to work in a very different way from that she has been used to. She feels that without the involvement of service-user partners, this learning just would not have taken place. She has also learned much from the local authority practitioners within the partnership. Jackie receives the genuine commitment on the part of all concerned to developing social workers and other qualified practitioners as *inspirational*.

The partnership works because all involved are totally committed to its process. The result is that much is learned by all.

Ed Morecroft and Sarah Craggs (see p.22) echo the lesson from EMAPP from the shared perspective of a social worker and a service user working together on an equal basis as co-trainers. For the two of them, it is the time spent working together and the regard they have for each other that enables this learning. They learn from one other 'by spending lots of time together in work and informal settings, by watching how each other deals with situations – over time we start to recognise each other's strengths and weaknesses.' Sarah makes Ed realise what it is possible for him to achieve – 'Never say never.' Ed makes Sarah question her own value base again and again. So when someone she supports wants to do something and Sarah may think it not possible, 'Ed will spring into her head.'

This *willingness* to see the contributions that each other can make and to examine and re-examine values is necessary in order for the richness of learning to be fully gained. Even when the relationship within the partnership is unequal, it is still possible to learn a great deal. Stephen describes how he learns from the people he assesses, who lack capacity:

> What matters is establishing people's values, beliefs and wishes and you need to come out of the assessment with these things intact. No two people are ever identical and you learn how to communicate with that individual on their terms. This will always involve consultation with others – professionals, friends and family – to get the wider picture. The point about individuality is critical and once I see a person I learn all about their beliefs and values; this essential part of them and who they are is what I take with me. They may be very poorly but they have still got their beliefs.

A belief in the value of other people and their uniqueness and what they can teach others is required in order to benefit from such abundant learning. Within partnerships, this requires professionals to acknowledge human strength and wisdom, especially where training and procedures might tend to focus on what people *can't* do. People using services might need to become more prepared to take risks and trust people, even when previous experience has perhaps been less than positive.

As Trish Green from A Place to Call our Own (APTCOO) reflects (see p.18), this willingness to take risks is borne by the strength gained from those first shared experiences with other families:

> We have a mutual understanding. We are able to acknowledge how we are feeling, and this process of mutual acknowledgement gives us the strength and tools to move forward. Members are able to give each other valuable information which helps us all and gives us starting points to find more information. We are able to encourage and support each other emotionally. We learn confidence from each other, which enables us to go out from the group to forge the other partnerships that will benefit our families and our group.

In summary

React and Sean's Final Journey show that everyone is both a teacher and a learner. The Long Distance Gang and Advocacy In Action celebrate the immense resources of wisdom and skills that accrue when partners work collectively together. PAct, however, warns against defining learning too narrowly or within restricted spaces, while EMAPP identifies the wealth of experience and skills within it and the benefits to individual members. Trish and APTCOO demonstrate the strength of peer learning where parents model both skills and qualities to one another.

A growing space is one where partners benefit from the richness of experience, different ways of thinking and understanding life that working with others brings. It is a space where this energy is celebrated and harnessed rather than being contained and divisive.

LEARNING FROM WORKING TOGETHER

Learning within partnerships not only comes from what other people teach us, but also from the very process of working together. Although it is Sean's illness that fully brings everyone together in partnership again, it is the previous Long Distance Gang journey to Ireland in 2008 that is the foundation of the strength now burgeoning within and around Sean. Nes reflects in 2010 that:

> ...while it is an emotional and turbulent time for all involved, it is also clear that the support given unquestioningly by members of the original group, and further by other men living in the hostel, is directly rooted

in The Long Distance Gang core values of mutual care and shared responsibility.

Julie recognises within manager Dave Milburn a complete and joyful openness to new learning, a humility in the face of lived experience and a burning commitment to bring colleagues with him. And Nes draws attention, not only to workers' increased understanding and dedication to their own role, but moreover to their new appreciation of their informal partners:

> …what is particularly noticeable during this period is a willingness by workers to understand the place of friends, allies and peers, as carers and supporters, with at least equally as valid an input in meeting social, cultural and well-being needs as anything health or care professions can offer.

Partners reflect jointly:

> We are now starting to discover some deep insights about death and dying and about 'letting go' in many ways. We are also coming together in our joint understandings of one another. We are learning to work as a stalwart team, discovering how to turn the risks over and find possibility green and growing. We are also coming to know how to be *vulnerable* together – which is so very, very important! We are learning from Sean himself how to step forward into this unknown terrain.

This learning together as a team is evidenced well through *React*'s partnership:

> The most important learning experience for all the children is building an understanding of 'voice'; through collaborative work, people can begin to express their views and preferences in different ways, enabling empowerment and equality. The pupils with learning and physical disabilities learn that they can have a dramatic impact on the world around them through communicating with their partners and others in different ways. The pupils from Colebourne Primary learn to see through their peers' disabilities, to view them not as 'disabled children' but 'friends' who happen to have a disability.

Advocacy In Action realises that members have learned lots of important lessons about human situations, recognising that many of their partners are trapped and helpless too. Kevin's wonderful picture – 'Patients and Staff Get Put Down by the Bosses' – says it all! It is in the bad spaces filled with bad power – where both workers and patients are oppressed – that people start to do bad things to one another. And the terrifying truth is that, even when the hospitals are uprooted, new bad spaces grow up in their place.

A worker draws his 'group home'. It is modern and purpose-built with landscaped gardens and a brightly painted door – but there are bars on the windows, and high railings surrounding the periphery. The worker says:

> ...this is what it feels like – the house where I work – there are no real bars and fence – although there might as well be, because we're all 'locked up' inside, by the rules and the culture as well as by the doors – we're all locked in – *I'm* trapped there too!'

It seems that we have much more in common with our partners in Advocacy In Action than we could ever have dreamed!

For June Sadd, the process of working within partnerships has taught her 'that each ally needs to be sensitive to the needs of the others to avoid alliances becoming tokenistic.' Service users and carers 'are more often than not bruised by their experiences, and although they are resilient, the impact of those experiences, whether recent or not, need to be seriously considered in any work together as allies.' For June, 'providers and commissioners *need to be* sensitive to the challenges by service users and carers which often focus on issues of care and control.' June believes that issues of power have to be acknowledged, as she has found in her experience that:

> ...learning to work together is not easy. Some allies find it more difficult working with the power imbalance and differential, firstly in acknowledging it and secondly in giving up their own power. There is much positive learning in all these aspects when alliances work well together and sadly much fallout when they do not.

PAct recognises that people do not necessarily enter into allegiances with the same motives or blueprints. Different agendas are around from the outset. PAct members know that people are not always compatible and can indeed collide! Funders and commissioners, accumulators of professional capital, hopefuls seeking a career boost, practitioners in pursuit of best practice, and all those freedom fighters and capacity-builders from the community and service-user groups, bump into one another and nudge for breathing space within the common ground of partnership.

An academic partner inhabiting one such teeming space sees how her own personal commitment to 'equally experienced values' conflicts with organisational loyalty to a university agenda. She recognises some 'pushing against normal university processes and structures' by the groups she is part of. In addition, she points to those good examples of power sharing that everyone learns from − joint responsibilities, recognitions, problem-solving, and some levelling of status within the groups. The tutor feels it is the ultimate willingness to work together that helps partners to navigate the stony bits and understand them. Members learn about partnership simply by 'getting on with it'!

Good partnership working does not automatically happen, however, even when people genuinely want it to work well. Real thought has to be given to the processes involved in people working together, and partnerships − particularly professionals working with service users − need to devote attention to the way in which they work.

Older People's Partnership Services (OPPS) partners (see p.27) have learned that people's skills and experience do not wither with age, but with careful tending, remain alive and growing. They reflect on their learning:

> ...my eyes have been opened and I believe I am wiser for being a part of OPPS. There has been much emotion involved for me − tears, anger, some laughter too. (Joyce Willard, older researcher partner)

> I have learned that older people have a strong voice about the type and quality of services that they may wish to access. I have learned that the skills learned in a person's younger life (work or living) do not necessarily disappear or become null and void, and that people are willing to use these skills long after work has ended. (Jullette Eaton Ruddock, local authority office partner)

> ...if we take time to listen, we can learn an awful lot. It's given me a renewed respect for older people. I now understand the importance of my role as a team assistant − we're an integral part of the division, helping to deliver the essential services. I now know I'd like to work more with older people. (Amita Naik, local authority officer partner)

> ...the group has recognised that they can all learn more from one another − everyone has different opinions, everyone has something

to offer. They have experienced the creative energy that comes from people in groups and seen how solidarity can be a mighty force. They have had common and shared purpose. Feeling safety in numbers, less-confident people have been helped to speak out. (Reshma Patel, group support partner; see p.31)

...being involved has been for me a humbling experience. I have learned a lot in relation to user involvement and participation. I have seen that the involvement of older people, working with other older people, makes such a difference to trust, confidence and empowerment. This has all given me huge job satisfaction. I feel really proud of how well the whole process and experience has worked and I believe that this is the only way forward. (Mary McCausland, local authority service director partner)

I've enjoyed meeting all the people. I've enjoyed the group and I've loved sharing news with everyone. We've had some laughs. And I've learned what's available for me in the future. I'm only 83 at present. I feel in a better position to handle what may lie ahead. (Ron Hayward, older researcher partner)

...it's common sense, but so easily disregarded by professionals who 'know better'. What an eye opener! Service-user feedback raises awareness – makes me realise that older people probably compromise far more than they should! It makes me realise that there may be more bad help than good in present service provision! Local authorities and providers – take note! If we don't ask, how do we know? (Wider policy-maker and provider partners)

Not bothering to ask – assuming answers – traps people in silos and dries them out. Working together in healthy growing spaces helps all sorts of partners learn about one another and about newer and freer ways of thinking and acting.

The Long Distance Gang members learn from their shared explorations through appreciative discussion. People discover that everyone's lives, experience and stories have value and appeal for others – even the 'taller' stories, such as Peter MacManaman's *Brief Encounter*! (Watch The Long Distance Gang film *Arise, You Gallant Sweeneys!* for more on this dodgy tale!) Partners realise the ability to learn new skills – photography, film-making, cookery – and the confidence to try them, through cultivating appreciation, hope and support for one another. New paths of problem-solving open themselves up, leaving that well-worn route to the bottle or the can somewhat less travelled.

Migrant work history of 'breakfast on the shovel', working 'on the lump' (cash in hand) and the power of Paddy's Prayer Book (*Construction News* weekly) both informs and is in turn informed by our deeper understanding of the injustices and coercions underlying it, and leads us to a discovery that we can all do more than just survive. We can respond and we can move on.

Dave Milburn sees that other residents resent The Long Distance Gang and are hostile to its members as they plan their trip to Ireland, but Sean tries to broaden understanding within the home:

> Sean is often willing and able to defend himself and his friends in times of open hostility, especially when too much alcohol has been consumed in the wider group. However, these situations provide an excellent opportunity for the Irish men to talk about their lives, culture and heritage with great pride and devotion. Staff feel that Julie has given men impetus and permission to celebrate their Irishness and experiences. Non-Irish residents in time acknowledge a degree of envy − it takes many weeks − envy that the Irish men's lives are somehow of great value and being celebrated.

As good experiences of joint partnership endorse, when thought is given to working together and the partnership works well, people learn much about others as well as about themselves. Sarah and Ed also share this closer knowledge of one another. They tell us what they learn through working together:

> I learn I can do more than I have been doing, a lot more – self-confidence – realising when services are holding me back. Getting a chance to do courses myself and find out about how services work. I can also let Sarah be part of my life at home – I never thought I would do that. I am used to keeping home and work very separate. (Ed)

> How important mutual respect is. Ed is like a barometer; I suggest things and he always comes back to me with an honest opinion. He helps me learn about how to hold an audience and about timing – he really is a natural performer. (Sarah)

For Stephen the lessons he learns from working with people who do not have capacity teach him about the preciousness of life and the many ways of understanding it:

> Some people have the gift of cherishing things and people, and this moves me. It also makes me stop and think that life is passing me by and shows me the value of the reflection on life that I see in others.

The value that comes from partnership working can go far beyond the partnership itself, as Stephen's example shows.

Reshma Patel and Sherma Patel (see p.31) learn to regard aspects of their own and each other's identity more positively. Sherma learns by working with Reshma that she has a really strong positive identity in relation to her disability. Reshma learns from Sherma how to sensitively 'help someone to address issues of identity in relation to race.'

In summary

Both OPPS and Sean's journey testify to the importance of peer educators, allies and supporters and of partners' willingness to learn. June reminds us that working together involves the giving up and sharing of power in order to be non-exploitative. And Sarah and Stephen both express deep humility as practitioners in what their partners have taught them.

In a growing space, the process by which partners work together is vitally important. People have to feel valued by how the partnership operates as much as by what it achieves.

WHAT HELPS AND WHAT HINDERS PARTNERSHIP WORKING?

The aggressiveness of Sean's treatment floors him. Weeks of radiotherapy, increasing medications and procedures have encroached on his precious time, leaving him weakened and frustrated. There are goals Sean wants to achieve in the months left to him, but differences of opinion among this partnership need to be reconciled. Those who 'stick by the book' feel threatened by some of the bigger plans being made – a '*boozy* birthday bash'? *Another* trip to *Ireland*? *Resident* involvement in their own and one another's care?

Dave and his team reflect on Sean's key role in helping his peers at '32' to partner him:

> Sean shares his life and his thoughts, feelings and experience in *his* way and on *his* level. Other residents can relate to a dying man – their friend – in a way staff would simply not be able to communicate. *These men all understand one another!* Other residents can also better understand what the staff are trying (and succeeding) to do. It feels incredibly unifying and empowering – probably uniquely so!

Dave muses on how partnership between staff and volunteers support Sean's plans: '...when radiotherapy becomes the next step, it is three dedicated volunteers who help Sean meet every session. They escort, sit with, stay with throughout.'

Dave considers if formal partners have become dependent on others, and wonders how:

> ...the team and some individuals would fare if Julie, Nes, and others were not part of the process. All staff agree we'd feel isolated perhaps. But I don't believe there is much evidence of our reliance on any one person at any one time. It is all shared, communicated and understood. Julie's genuine desire to consult, share and learn is most palpable.

In Dave's opinion, the partners are bound not by dependency, but by trust.

The fact that everyone *wants* the Asperger's Consultation Group (see p.20) to succeed is a definite factor in its success. This motivation in turn leads to commitment, focus and respect for each other. The tasks necessary to achieve together are broken down into 'manageable chunks' and the group travels at a pace that is right for everyone. Lack of pressure to work in a certain way or to a given timescale – or to be assigned tasks that make people feel uncomfortable or pressured – are all cited by the group as very important to them.

OPPS benefits from the independence of Advocacy In Action workers. It helps them both to be value-centred and process-centred and to work towards shared ownership from the start. Leicester City Council's support, from cabinet lead and service director to community officer and team assistant, is equally important, validating and motivating. The sheer enthusiasm and wonderful pooled resources of the older researchers and their subjects make up the third side within this triangle of possibility.

Hindrances involve external constraints such as time pressures, the need to be Criminal Records Bureau (CRB) checked and problems arranging cash expenses. And there are additional internal tensions, which include contractual wrangles, sharing of budget information and other tools of power, and little patches of 'competitiveness' and lack of cooperation from officers who feel their territory invaded or compromised by the group. Within the membership of OPPS itself, there are some differences of understanding and levels of support. Going at a slow pace frustrates those who are able to latch on quicker. People also get fed up when they feel others aren't 'pulling their weight.' Some male members do not get the same warmth of reception and are perceived to be 'there for all the wrong reasons.' Levels of confidence and self-esteem among OPPS members are easily knocked. Finally, a hiatus between planning and preparation and the research action phase totally deflates everyone and threatens to sap the good energy within the group. OPPS, however, is able to *reflect on and learn from* both its hindrances and helps – to own their outcomes, and to proceed forward with optimism and assurance.

While Long Distance Gang members benefit from the spaces they create at '32', there *are* problems. Other residents are increasingly frustrated at the level of interest and the nature of the partnership. Muttered grumblings and derision still mask resentment – 'Why are *they* getting all the attention?' And there is also a danger of territorialism, with some workers feeling the urgency to control. One in particular is quite protective of her plans with Tom. *She* wants to be the person who takes him home to Ireland. Does such an imperative to 'manage' spring from organisational or from personal need, or does one mask the other? There is a sense that 'partnership' for some practitioners is more about validating role and purpose within work, in particular, where similar activities are in place, rather than creating something truly shared and owned.

But the distances close up as more and more of '32's' residents come to feel part of The Long Distance Gang's space, whether or not part of the forthcoming journey. Gatherings take on a gentle sort of sharing, as newcomers just move their chairs in a little closer. The Long Distance Gang became an open place for workers to take time out and for friends to drop in.

Dave re-captures:

> ...the great sense of anticipation and excitement just before the trip — The Long Distance Gang gives staff a good buzz. The day before the departure there is a team meeting, where staff feel pride in 'staying with the plan' and seeing something through to conclusion — not just an aside or a 'good idea', but a real collective who have nurtured us all and implanted ambition and hope.

For Reshma and Sherma, power differentials have been a factor in hindering them early on in their partnership, but as they explore this, it becomes a factor that strengthens the relationship. Reshma summarises the issues:

> ...the fact that at first we don't know each other, power differentials, time and resources have definitely been a hindrance. The main thing that helps this partnership grow is that Sherma recognises that she can learn from me *and* vice versa. It also helps that we like each other and furthermore can recognise each other's limitations to what we can offer the partnership.

In spite of Advocacy In Action's positive values and genuine enthusiasm for one another, tiny pockets of bad power hinder its beginnings. Kevin, Brian and Julie recall the early meetings:

> ...there are still some dodgy power differences among members — almost a hierarchy. Those with severe learning and mental health difficulties are pushed to the bottom. Intellect is valued over emotion. Some partners are also very racist and 'anti-gay'. There are assumptions about the roles men and women should occupy in the group. Participants look up to the 'most capable' — want to put them in positions of power. It feels very difficult at times. Members ignore one another in a rush to make contact with and impress professional visitors. We suppose this is the reaction to a lifetime of being trodden down. But learning to stand up tall, strong and proud, only seems to tempt certain people to want to take on the more 'powerful roles' for themselves — even if it means treading on colleagues. We need to sort this stuff out together!

So Advocacy In Action begins to encourage people of 'difference' to work together, in creative ways that will promote mutual support, respect and admiration. Within the group, people are encouraged to partner themselves up with those whom they know less about. And within public events, it is not always the 'most powerful' who front the proceedings. Advocacy In Action finds room for everyone to witness, to be witnessed and to contribute, in ways that turn notions of 'inability' and 'neediness' on their head.

It is also important to reflect how 'outside' people support or hinder partnership work for Advocacy In Action in the early days. We still tell the story of a social services chair who, in 1990, sends the following message out to every team in her local authority:

Have Nothing to Do With this Group!

And we recall how the day services staff manipulated service users' timetables so they couldn't get to Advocacy In Action meetings, cajoled people to leave because 'all this busy activity is doing you no good', and maintained a professional eye on 'suspect' Advocacy In Action activity, setting up the 'Advocacy In Action Monitoring Group!'

Parents and parent groups too have concerns and worries when sons and daughters start to speak for themselves: '…no girl of mine is going to give me cheek!' says 92-year-old Dolly of her 60-year-old disabled daughter Pam. Some even gatecrash our meetings to argue, plead or pull their family members out. All to no avail! It just makes the partners ever more determined to keep the group going.

It should be stressed that those who hinder are a minority. Advocacy In Action has a growing body of support.

Early partners take real risks in openly celebrating what we stand for. However, all trust is rewarded when the service-user movement sweeps us up on a wave of collective belief and energy. It is our time. We have arrived. We celebrate with our allies when we win big national awards as trainers and community leaders.

Meanwhile, where are the erstwhile detractors? Nowhere to be found! Suddenly it seems that *everyone* wants to have *everything* to do with this group. Directors want to pick up awards with the partners. Officers sing their praises at conferences. Happiest of all is a meeting with the most vocal of the parent-antagonists, one year later in 1991, when, no longer here to oppose, he applauds in tears as his own daughter takes the stage.

Twenty years on and the involvement of service users and carers is widely accepted, and it is recognition of function and dedicated funding that now help EMAPP and other formal partnerships. Participants can now be properly valued, reimbursed and rewarded. Previous strong relationships among university, local authority and service-user members ease participants into a shared purpose when these forums are set up. As previously identified, the *willingness* to work together is most helpful to everyone.

Time is an important factor and it is necessary 'to establish relationships leading to power sharing and trust in the early stages of partnerships.' Time spent together exploring issues of identity is clearly important for Advocacy In Action and equally for Sherma and Reshma's partnership. But time is sometimes a luxury that people don't have. EMAPP agendas are pressed for time, as busy partners dash in and out.

Stephen Vickers (see p.32) finds it crucial that he uses his time well, with any person whom he assesses. He has learned ways to maximise this:

> As a result of working together, you have an idea of what is in a person's best interests. This might at times still feel uncomfortable as the decision being made may not be the decision the person wants to hear at that moment. There is a diversity of how people understand the world and the most effective way of communicating is to try and link to things that interest them. Working with people has shown me the wealth of different ways of interpreting the world and some of the pleasures that people take in simple things.

This focusing on what is important to the person and trying to understand their perspective is not only helpful to the person Stephen is assessing, but also gives him much in return: 'You gain a better understanding of your own world and this is a gift that people have given me.'

Advocacy In Action members have experience of 'reluctant' partnerships, where, for example, the outcomes are unwanted, but the journey towards them is positive and dignified. Julie recalls a co-worker whose children are placed in care, but who thanks the worker involved for their honesty and their sensitivity, for making the journey towards the inevitable more bearable, and for sharing information and decision-making, thus helping her reclaim some control at a difficult time.

Then again, there are the positive spaces that can grow in the most restricted of surroundings, such as the collaboration between serving prisoners in Maghaberry maximum security jail in County Antrim and artists, in the acting and filming of *Mickey B*, the hard man's version of Macbeth.

What helps both these partnerships to blossom is the emphasis first and foremost on people's humanity and what they have to bring to the situation.

Ed and Sarah realise the very human fact that they like each other helps with their partnership. They find that shared humour and banter and teasing each other play an important part in their relationship. This helps to overcome Ed's history of being let down by people, although their partnership needed to develop slowly at first because of this. It will not always be that, when working in different alliances, everyone will like each other as much as Sarah and Ed, however. Individuals should be mindful of the previous experience of others, and realise when it may affect their willingness to trust. Nevertheless, as Ed has shown, even where people have been let down in previous partnerships, it is still possible for them to move on, providing they can meet with more positive and nurturing experiences.

In summary

Growing spaces are truly creative in recognising the opportunities hidden within the obstacles and being undeterred when the ground is stony.

WHO MAKES THE DECISIONS?

There is a lot of talk about 'shared decision-making' in partnerships, but just how true is this?

Many Long Distance Gang decisions are jointly shared and owned by all partners. There are constraints, however. First, there is the issue of capacity when too much ale and strong cider has been imbibed. Decisions are conveniently 'forgotten' after a bender. So meetings have to be held early morning, while heads are reasonably 'unfuddled'. And writing agreements down helps everyone remember.

The Long Distance Gang also faces 'safeguarding' restrictions on some members. Care regimes are rigid and unbending. The ethos at '32', however, encourages shared decision-making where possible. Manager Dave Milburn promotes a brave vision of 'well-being' that dares to be different and enables older men to have wings and fly if they choose to.

Some partners don't want the responsibility. 'You decide!' they say to others. But The Long Distance Gang asks that everyone agrees or disagrees with what is being discussed and the decisions reached. Over time, more people become more involved in making decisions, big and small. And there is a shared respect for all decisions within the partnership, whether they belong to the group or to individuals.

Dave reflects on one man's difficult decision: '…it is sad to see and accept that Tom Coffey is not willing, and perhaps not able to make the trip — but his feeling and thoughts are accepted as his own and respected nonetheless.' Tom's suitcase is packed. He has Euros in his pocket. But at the last minute he decides not to go. Is it the cold ashes — too many lonely sad years since the 14-year-old 'man of the house' migrated to the UK to support his widowed mother and family? Or maybe in the facing of what lies ahead, in the burning anger he owes to a crafty younger brother whom Tom suspects has stolen the farm in his absence? Whatever the reasons, Tom's decision is his own, and his partners can only reassure him that he is still very much part of the journey in spirit and an essential, albeit absent, member of the Gang.

The Long Distance Gang feels it is not always about *who* makes the decisions but about *how* people are respected, involved and supported within the processes. Nes and Julie discuss how decision-making is made more attractive and accessible for everyone by:

> …the open nature of meetings, the primary social aspects, the time given to enable ideas to germinate at their own pace and in their own way – the forging of this communal growing space — physical space but also a space for thinking and feeling, for everyone to throw in their own ideas.

Some Leicester City Council decisions are not wholly supported by OPPS members, such as the requirement to CRB check the older researchers and the big scheduling alterations. However, '…we have to know which windmills to tilt at and which to let ride. Major decisions over ownership of the findings are the ones we head into with all our energies focused.' Research consultant Julie Gosling knows where her own negotiating skills are best placed and targets them appropriately!

Regarding the OPPS' research itself, the task is set by the local authority's requirement. Mary needs to evaluate how older service users have received an outcome-based home support pilot, and how effective the service promises to be. However, all further processes are genuinely owned by researchers.

In any partnership, individuals within it have specific roles, but how do these roles get assigned and who assigns them? This is a key point for June. She reflects on the disappointing experience of instances where:

> Unfortunately the decision about roles has not been shared between the allies either through deliberate manipulation or mainly because the power-holders didn't 'get it' at first. Sadly in many instances the alliances then become tokenistic. Much of the initial work together needs to be to establish the principle of 'shared responsibility'. Roles do not have to be assigned in traditional ways. The chair does not have to be the most powerful person in the room. With support the role can be taken by someone with less power or perhaps there could be two co-chairs modelling shared responsibility.

PAct members learn from experience that equality and democracy do not always equal unanimous agreement – everyone has their own agendas! And, furthermore, collaboration does not always equal democracy or equality! PAct recall an occasion where Gina infamously puts 'partnership' on trial at a large social work conference, accusing it of duplicity and power-mongering and asking the professional audience to act as jury in deliberating the motives and the integrity of the defendant!

It would be lovely to say that everyone makes all the decisions all the time, but of course this isn't so. However, what Advocacy In Action can honestly say is that where people *want* to join in, they are supported to do so.

> We never meet a human being who is not able to play their part in decision-making. But it is our partner Ailish who most embodies this when we meet her in 1996 during tenant participation events in West London. Ailish uses noises and sounds. She is carried from her wheelchair to the sofa. Two workers are there to feed her, change her, to help her join in. One less caring worker comments that Ailish's presence serves no purpose: '…she can't speak – can't understand – she's always asleep when I bring her out!' Another worker sees more in Ailish. By acting as Ailish's voice, she helps her to retaliate: 'I *choose* the company I keep, by opening and closing my eyes!'

As APTCOO develops, Trish recalls that:

> …two purposes of the group emerge. The first half of our meetings tend to be sharing and mutual support and the second half come to be a focus on talking about reaching out to other parents about their needs,

views and their lives and *what are their* issues. And thus, we end up with a wish list from other parents. Between all the parents we are in touch with a lot of different professionals and services. The shared knowledge from this helps to put together this wish list. The contact we have with other parents helps us realise that we are not on our own and that other families have similar lives and face similar challenges. This knowledge gives us the confidence and impetus to move forward. This is like a snowball growing and we can no longer fit into the room we have been allocated. We go to Mansfield CVS [Community and Voluntary Service] with our wish list and ask for advice on how to move forward. The CVS are really helpful. During this process the parents in our group develop roles according to their skills and what they feel comfortable doing.

For APTCOO, the shared responsibility clearly comes from a common purpose and the 'wish list' that captures the dreams and ambitions of the families for a better future. From this naturally come forward individuals who are willing and keen to take on specific roles. This is not always the way partnerships develop, however. For Sarah and Ed, decision-making changes as Ed grows in confidence:

> ...it has changed over time – at first it's Sarah. Now Ed decides what work he is and is not doing and decides whether he needs help with it. Sometimes he does – other times he goes solo.

The Asperger's Consultation Group agree roles according to what people are good at and willing to do: 'We rely on our skills sets. We do what we feel comfortable doing. Everyone decides what they are comfortable to do.' Such flexibility is crucial for this partnership as it avoids unnecessary pressure, and the members of the Group feel free to develop their chosen skills in much the same way as the APTCOO parents.

EMAPP roles are also decided by negotiation, albeit achieved in a more formal way through meetings. Mick describes how roles are assigned through 'open discussion at a number of forums with volunteers enlisted to work on all areas of the programme.' Admittedly there are occasions when similar people do volunteer.

The process of assigning roles differs according to the type of partnership. For quite a formal partnership such as EMAPP, different individuals in the partnership carry different responsibilities. This does partly dictate the roles people take on within it. Mick comments: that 'some naturally fall to academic partners and some to service-user or agency partners. It has always been important to consistently check out agreement and understanding of roles between partners.' So, even when individual roles seem clear, it is still important to negotiate their detail. Certainly within this particular partnership, each partner enriches and assists the roles of others, by bringing in fresh perspectives.

The Asperger's Consultation Group and EMAPP are both partnerships where discussion has helped to agree roles. However, for Sarah and Ed, it is a much more organic process: '…it has just evolved – if Ed was ever to feel himself carrying too much responsibility too soon, he would say 'no'. He's needed to realise for himself that he is up to the job.'

Anil reflects within PAct on what has helped and hindered his partnership work:

> My professional colleagues and I *do* work well together and see possibilities on the horizon for real collaboration, blossoming from our mutual regard for and trust in one another. However, we are told there isn't the money to go any further. All of us are gutted! We feel that a good partnership between us has not been allowed to grow, even though there is big potential for it. I am aware it has been inhibited by outside influences. This 'partnership' to date has been definitely task oriented, and now that the task is completed there is no longer a requirement for the partnership to continue, regardless of what it could still achieve. As a disabled man, I have experienced this so many times, I have come to expect it as a 'given'. I feel there is an important lesson here. It is that organisations initiating partnerships should be clear right from the start, if there *is* an end point in view – that *this* is what is going to happen and *this* will be where the partnership stops. It would save us building up our hopes and making plans that can never see fruition.

Cancer makes some choices for Sean and his supporters. But within what remains, Sean makes both wise and unwise decisions, while partners build a supportive net around them. Dave describes how 'Sean always leads the way for us – we protect his decisions.' Sean and Julie share ideas to meet Sean's hopes and dreams. Before he dies, Sean wants to make a third and final visit to Arvagh in County Cavan, to say goodbye. He plans to join Julie at the University of Nottingham for one last teaching session. He tells Julie that he hopes to celebrate their shared birthday in style. He wants to have more contact with his daughter Gaynor. And he has an unrealised longing to go to the ballet. Most of his plans need to be brought forward as Sean takes a turn for the worse. Nes agrees to help them get to Ireland before Christmas.

Sean's plans meet with resistance from many quarters. There are workers at '32' who will not let go and who want to manage Sean and his illness through safer routes. They are focused on physical care and pain management. The GP threatens that pain control will not be upped while Sean continues to drink. Sean refuses to listen and goes without pain relief, which leads to sleepless nights for himself and others.

When Stephen assesses people, the roles are fixed, in that he is fulfilling a statutory duty. But within this, he recognises how essential it is to adapt how he carries out his role in accordance with the needs of the person:

> At some point during the assessment you need to explain what exactly you are exploring with them. In some cases you might have to break down the question into bite-size pieces. The role you play is dictated by how the person is – each assessment is different. We must never have a blanket approach and we never stick to one way of working or a time frame – it is all bespoke according to the service user.

In summary

June warns against assumptions of capacity or lack of it and Advocacy In Action's account of Ailish's involvement testifies to this. The Long Distance Gang, Advocacy In Action and OPPS all model shared responsibility in decision-making as well as recognising that not all decisions need necessarily include everyone. PAct reflects that equality and democracy do not always equal concordance. And Anil, for PAct, mourns the important decisions not shared with service users that then go on to affect outcomes in partnerships. Finally, Sean throws out the challenge of the right to decide – wisely or unwisely.

In a growing space everyone has the opportunity to contribute to decisions. The final decision might have to be made by one person, but that is after other partners have been listened to and their opinions carefully considered.

HOW DO PARTNERSHIPS AGREE ON THEIR VISION?

...not least, absolutely not least — the last trip to Ireland — a magnificent fusion of ambition and desire. The coming together of Julie, Nes, Sean, Macmillan nurse Caroline McCluskey, and staff at '32' interlink to create a virtually seamless adventure.

So Dave recalls the united vision that sweeps Sean, Julie and Nes to Ireland in December 2010.

Money is raked in from Framework Housing, Macmillan, FIANN (a local Irish volunteer network) and The Fifty Fund, drawing in old and new financial partners. The GP writes a letter of information and support to assist with any treatment required while away. The drugs box is packed to the brim.

Sean, Julie and Nes are looking firmly ahead and everyone follows in their wake.

Shared elements, at least, of any vision are important when planning to work together with others. Knowing how to get there also requires some thought.

It is Advocacy In Action's custom to draw up a partnership 'compact' of *how* they intend to work with people, before they get down to the practicalities of *what* they plan to produce.

> We always aim for a range of outcomes relating to process as well as to the 'end project'. What we have found in the past, however, is that although agreements are signed up to, they are somehow ambiguous and dependent on context. How do you 'listen with respect' when someone is doing their best to squash you? How easy is it to feel 'free to challenge appropriately' when you are in mental or spiritual distress? How can you even begin to agree 'not to make or condone discriminatory remarks' when your understanding of the dynamics of oppression are limited? We try not to sign up to what we can't fulfil.

'Going home' is what migrants long for, and the Irishmen in The Long Distance Gang are no exception. But it is recognised that for some, after absences of many years, and with little in their pockets to account for their severances, getting home will be very, very hard indeed. Nevertheless, 'going home' *is* the ultimate collective vision for The Long Distance Gang.

Sean, Tom and Pat do not share any such dreams at first. After the alcohol kicks in, they are simply happy to steer backwards in time towards shadowy memories of familiar places.

Dave holds to a vision of emancipation, where the men at '32' might break the chains of their alcoholism and have 'better lives' to look forward to.

In a sense, the final vision is imported in, and this is a dilemma that Julie and Nes have to own. Each navigates to their own horizon. For Julie, it is the fulfilling of dreams and longings of the 'forgotten' within her own community. Nes looks to the lives of those who have been forced to leave or flee. Both identify how issues of power can cloud and obscure the way forward.

Nes deliberates on the quandary that:

> ...in any current debate or discussion around migration, or indeed, any issue regarding marginal, forgotten or invisible communities, discussion inevitably takes place between those in positions of relative power — be they politician, academic, practitioner, activist, or artist — and *not* in consultation or partnership with those communities — as has ever been the case.

Julie considers how:

> ...others create the vision and then bring in the 'disadvantaged and distressed' to empower them — but well intentioned groups and folk can have a way of only focusing on what *they* want to see.

Trish reflects on a conscious process of reaching the shared APTCOO vision through the original 'wish list' early families had written. It is a crucial vehicle for the group's development:

> Our shared vision becomes the aims and objectives of the charity and when we come under the Charity's Commission we have to maintain this vision. We are very focused as we want the project to succeed and we are *scared* of doing anything wrong. This helps us focus and resist attempts from outside influences to change or compromise our vision.

This very conscious and carefully thought through vision is necessary for the formation of a new charity like APTCOO, but a vision of a partnership is not always as *openly* discussed or acknowledged. Talking of EMAPP, Jeanette comments: 'I might think that we all have a shared vision; however, if you ask each one of us to describe that vision you will get I am sure lots of different answers.'

Sarah and Ed are used to working in a way that identifies goals and they use it to help them clarify their vision of working together: 'We do a PATH – a type of person-centred plan – and then we work towards the goals set in this.'

Not everyone carries positive experiences of building shared visions in partnerships. In talking about a shared vision, June has had experiences that have taught her that this is not always an equal process: 'I would say that it is often a compromise with the less powerful having to give more ground.'

In summary

Advocacy In Action and The Long Distance Gang point to the importance of process as well as end point when creating shared visions. Nes and Julie discuss the inevitability of visions often being 'owned' by power-holders. June too warns that shared vision may actually mask an incorporation of the less powerful.

In a growing space, different visions can co-exist and make room for one another.

HOW ARE DIFFERENT PERSPECTIVES VALUED?

The formal eyes of Leicester City Council see things very differently to its older service users and citizens, while activists Julie and Reshma bring another slant. Not all perspectives can be accommodated at all times and this causes conflict both between people and inside of people. Team assistant Amita Naik often finds herself pulled two ways – torn between professional loyalty and personal commitment to the older people. For Mary too, her belief in the values laid down by the researchers is sometimes tempered by resource or policy constraints. Julie often finds herself reigned in by bureaucracy, while Reshma's own dependence on services keeps silent at times when she knows she should speak out. By being honest and open with our outlooks and the factors that accommodate or compromise them, we reach a 'satisficing' of perspectives which is somewhere between satisfy and suffice. Understanding where other people are coming from and the conflicts they face helps us to value their inputs. Everyone can then move towards a point where they can move forward together.

The Asperger's Consultation Group finds that having no specific leader means they feel more equal and this leads to a sense that different perspectives are valued. They also point to the behaviour of people in meetings as promoting this. Group members, always polite and respectful, listen to what people have to say, rather than talking across each other.

The behaviour of the individual EMAPP members also demonstrates that different perspectives are valued. Jeanette explains:

> I think this question is determined by the fact that everyone has a commitment to solving the problem and respect for each other – we all treat each other well and remember to value difference and diversity.

Although service-user, community, professional and academic perspectives are often equally well regarded, PAct says this does not necessarily mean that accommodating them is easy. Julie describes an invitation to speak at a gathering, where she submits the title and description of her proposed topic for the conference. Imagine her feelings on the day when, in the official programme, she finds her words soft-soaped and watered down, with all the wallop and polemic washed out of them!

PAct asks itself a further question – are service user groups as entirely inclusive as they would like to believe? Service users are not immune from enquiry when it comes down to how they treat one another.

> And although we like to believe, as people 'on the receiving end', that our shared experiences produce in us some shared sense of perspective, are we, as service users and carers, always fully sensitive to *everyone's* situation, regardless of how it manifests?

Kevin recalls the fear caused by a co-worker who deals with frustration and anxiety through aggressive words and gestures. The man is avoided, until peers recognise the feelings behind the fist of the man, who has learned in an institution that negative attention is better than none. Colleagues soon find ways to help transform the shake of his fist into a friendly wave. He is then supported within a formal partnership (although he does still give it the occasional two fingers!).

Members of PAct reflect that diversity has many facets and perspectives, some of which are hidden to them.

Advocacy In Action is just like a blackberry (the fruit, not the phone!), with a different view reflected in each tiny sphere. Every miniature world is equally important in contributing to the whole. The partners love all the worlds that others bring to them, so Advocacy In Action cultivates a composite vision to accommodate everyone's experience.

> We find out about each other and try to glimpse all these realities from our different perspectives. But what if a view is distorted or damaged? We can only try to understand how it came to be so and offer kinder, healthier perspectives to balance or remedy it. And if any outlook is so blighted that it risks poisoning the whole group, then it has to go.

So when a nurse lecturer insists on imposing her ideas onto Advocacy In Action, and will only speak to the members she considers 'equal', it damages all of the partners. They try very hard to help correct this, but the nurse lecturer won't consider any other viewpoint. In the end, with some sadness, the person is cut out.

Parents bring their own perspectives that may seem to work against the partners. Advocacy In Action therefore tries to finds ways to unite and work together with parents and carers. At a workshop in Oxfordshire, in 1994, a mother wheels her daughter in to meet the group: 'I am Elizabeth's ears, I am Elizabeth's eyes, I am Elizabeth's mind,' she tells us. 'I *am* Elizabeth!' We spend a weekend together – 'Looking Back With Love – Looking Forward With Hope.' We help Pamela untangle herself from her daughter to see how unique and precious both of them are. A different mother leaves with her daughter, declaring: 'we *may* be carer and dependant – and we *may* be mother and daughter – but first and foremost, we are two women, and *neither* of us are getting our needs met!'

On another day, it is a father, Malcolm, who challenges Advocacy In Action's viewpoint. He rubbishes the idea of self-advocacy: 'It's okay for you lot,' he sneers to the members with learning disabilities, 'you're *more* than my son – you're all walkers and talkers – but you're still a load of puppets – don't tell me that there isn't someone somewhere pulling the strings!'

> Of course, this hurts us and, more than hurt, it offends us. But we look at a father with his son and try to view things through the eyes of someone who is constantly being told by the experts that his son is a bunch of problems and special needs that can never be mended. And then Malcolm is assisted to see and own the great beauty within

his son, Michael, and to celebrate the love between them. When other proud parents and carers shout out all their sons and daughters' 'special strengths', Malcolm sits hand in hand with Michael. At last, tears streaming down his face, he begs people not to think him stupid, as he whispers the joy and pride of seeing Michael step onto a bus unaided.

Some of this sharing is brave indeed – full of pain, resilience, survival, joy and hope. It is surely the multifaceted complexity that makes these encounters such perceptive growing spaces.

Although many perspectives are involved in assisting The Long Distance Gang in getting to Ireland, they cannot all be incorporated with the same priority. A 'person-centred' ethos dictates that travellers will see one another as *people first*. But a more traditional care focus skews thinking at times and serves to put a negative slant on preparation. So when the minibus-cum-pub-on-wheels is packed with lovely necessary provisions – Special Brew, Irish Whisky in the roof space, boxes of cigarettes, cassettes and edibles under the seats – the sly plastic aprons and disposable gloves that slip their way into the luggage have to be thrown out again in disgust: '…either we *all* wear them or *nobody* wears them.' So back to the care home they go!

> The Long Distance Gang have agreed to look after one another, and we do this very responsibly, including help with medication and catheters. But we do to one another as fellow travellers rather than as carers and the cared-for.

Notwithstanding the little tensions caused by disparity between perspectives, it has to be said that a remarkable unity emerges within this partnership and there is mutual learning from all the points of view of the others. Service users recognise the worker responsibilities and volunteers appreciate the bigger organisational picture. Care staff from '32' enthuse at broader and more positive ways of relating to people and learn that risk-taking is not something to shy away from. This results in better spaces for working together and ensures that the perspectives guiding the journey to Ireland are balanced and buoyant.

The haste and direction of Sean's illness in 2010 demand that differing viewpoints accommodate one another to support a true person-centred approach. 'I believe the partnership is finding its hold and its depth,' observes Dave, as increasingly more partners focus on meeting Sean's wishes, although not everyone is on board and obstacles are still placed in the way. But the concerns underlying resistance to the journey are recognised and respected, and then put in their place. This is difficult for some. One worker is so wrapped up in it that she invites herself along to administer medication. Sean refuses, however, and insists that he will choose who goes with him. When the worker 'capitulates', it is to decisions already made without her. But she is supported to feel part of them, and enabled to become enthusiastic for the travellers.

Stephen highlights the importance of values and respecting people's perspectives in the work that he does:

> It is important not to jump to conclusions and not to judge. It is about respecting that person as an individual and respecting that we all come from different backgrounds. It is important to try and put yourself in people's circumstances.

In assessing a person with less or no capacity, it is this valuing of their perspective that actually forms the basis of the assessment. Professionals who assess people in this circumstance need to make every effort to understand what decision they might make for themselves if they had capacity. This can only be done by really trying to understand people both as they are now and as they were.

React achieved this accommodating of views with the pupils by encouraging them 'to acknowledge each other's perspectives through exploring preferences and allowing each other to make choices.'

Sarah and Ed emphasise the importance of just talking issues through:

> We talk – often informally in a café, the car – we always debrief at the end of training, sometimes the next day if we need to. We each use another colleague [same one], to chat through any major concerns we have before talking them through together.

In summary

OPPS show how different perspectives bend to accommodate one another, although PAct warns that not all may be equally valued within all partnerships. Advocacy In Action reflects on the diversity of worlds that different partners experience and bring with them, and Stephen names the importance of remaining open to everyone's views on life.

In a growing space, partners learn how others see the world differently. Their own understandings are broadened and more informed and enriched decisions can be made.

HOW IS DIFFERENT EXPERIENCE VALUED IN PARTNERSHIPS?

For many, 'different' feels like second class: 'I have met with more wisdom and intelligence on a building site than in many a university.' So Julie reproves the 'grey-heads' of The Long Distance Gang, when they dismiss their own precious lives as rubbish! Most of them, she realises, have little schooling. Many know the demands of child labour. They see small value in their own lives or experience and do not readily accept what others glimpse in them. So one of the major challenges is to create safe, appreciative spaces, where partners can cherish themselves as well as others, focusing on life knowledge and on personal qualities.

The very fact that people are being interviewed and filmed shows them how valued their stories are. Time spent together, listening, sharing, laughing and weeping is the stuff of shared experience, and crosses the boundaries of age, culture, gender and circumstance. And although only certain stories are for filming, the exchanges within The Long Distance Gang demand that *everyone* gives freely of themselves – cooks, whistle players, drivers, bottle washers, film participants, film-makers, drinkers and 'pioneers!'

The giving and receiving of experience measures the value it is now starting to hold for everyone. This will extend, on return to England, into the making and showing of the film and further still into public speaking by the older Irish men (cans and fags in hand) at the local university.

When diversity is valued in a partnership it has the power to make the partnership much stronger. Different partnerships say that not only does diversity define the partnership, it is, moreover, the *dynamic* that makes it effective. PAct speaks out against what Reshma eloquently describes as the tick-box requisitioning of her ethnicity and disability to point-score!

The Asperger's Consultation Group sees the different experiences in the group as a real asset and group members often acknowledge this verbally. The fact that people are different ages and have different experiences of life and of living with Asperger's means they can learn from each other, and together can understand a wider range of experience within the Asperger's community. This is very useful for the research they are engaged in. Members summarise this: 'The project needs a wide perspective and the diversity of the group brings this. We are stronger as a team than as individuals.'

Trish, too, identifies the importance of diversity in APTCOO's early days:

> The diversity is an asset as it makes us not be enclosed in our own 'bubble' and makes us aware of what is happening in the voluntary sector and also it helps us understand how to do things properly. We are very aware we have a lot to learn and so we really value the opportunity to learn from other people's experience. It also opens doors to funding opportunities. First, fund raising and awareness in the community, and secondly, fund raising bids and statutory funding. We are helped with both of these.

The diversity of experience and knowledge of the members of APTCOO and of the partners they begin to work with in the voluntary sector enable APTCOO to grow and start to achieve its wishes for children with disabilities and their families.

EMAPP also believes that it is the different perspectives that make the partnership a success. Jeanette comments: 'The diversity among us has made the group successful. It has always been valued.'

The professional experience of '32' workers and the healthcare practitioners is highly valued by Julie and Nes. It helps them to feel confident with the routines they will need to administer while in Ireland, particularly around opiates, liquid nutrition and catheter management. Sean, reluctantly admits that the pain relief enabled by care staff is crucial to his well-being, but he insists that nothing, pain included, is going to get in the way of his return to Ireland.

The importance of 'going home' for Sean, as an Irishman, is deeply respected by Julie and Nes, and Dave encourages his team to understand and support them.

The experience of pain and illness and how to live with it is something everyone learns from. Sean's determination to do things his own way overrides his suffering. And it is actually the point at which Nes and Julie throw policy to the wind and commit to be guided by Sean.

Sarah and Ed explain how their diversity is the key to their success as trainers:

> We could not deliver the training we do in Nottinghamshire now without it − Ed's experience and perspective is what makes people listen. Sarah's technical knowledge helps people learn 'how' to approach something but it is Ed's input that gives it heart and emotion and makes people want to try Sarah's ideas.

Back to the Advocacy In Action 'blackberry' again! All our experience is unique, rich, luscious, wherever we nibble. Experience is the life juice of Advocacy In Action.

> It enables our very existence as a group and courses through all of our partnerships. We believe in the power of storytelling as a way of spreading experience to enrich understanding. We tell our stories within books, pictures and films. But nothing is quite so powerful as the personal sharing, described by one student listener, as 'face-to-face-nowhere-to-hide confrontation'.

Advocacy In Action acknowledge that everyone has a story and that all stories deserve to be told and heard. For it is through storytelling that we reclaim our experience. So within partnerships they ask that stories are received with respect and humility. Telling the story is both healing and validating and allows partners to face forwards and upwards from the strong roots of their experience. Their stories are received by practitioners and learners and help them in turn to tap into their own:

> I think in the past, I have blotted out my own experience and it has been very unhealthy for me. I can see how I am not working to the best of my abilities and how this negatively impacts on the people I work with. I can see how your trust in me opens me up − just like I know I can trust in and listen to future service users. It opens my eyes to people's essential knowledge and wisdom, and to an understanding that service users will need to feel safe and trust me. This trust is a two-way street.

Advocacy In Action see that different experiences − shared and valued − unite us along very common parameters. They not only enrich and inform one another, but can also actually help us see what binds us together. It is the exchange of experience between service users and service providers that enables Advocacy In Action in 1998 to develop a fresh understanding of both as *shared survivors* in social control systems. We start to spread this new idea to partners and allies and within teaching and training spaces. People pick up the seeds and carry their ideas even further.

In summary

Diversity can be exploited by less scrupulous partners as a tick-box exercise, PAct warns. However, both the Asperger's Consultation Group and The Long Distance Gang recognise and celebrate diversity as a defining and dynamic element within their partnerships.

Within a growing space, different experiences are valued as being equally valid. Allies recognise that without different experiences, partnerships would be much poorer.

POWER DIFFERENCES

While it is clear that diversity within partnerships can be a huge asset to them, there are invariably differences of power between different people within any partnership. How these relationships are managed is another factor in determining their success.

PAct recognises that all alliances accommodate patches of good *and* bad power and that we can all find ourselves wading through either at different times within any partnership. There is no clear definition of 'powerful' or 'powerless' within the roles and capacities held by various members, and the majority experience feelings of both strength and ineffectiveness, regardless of how they may be perceived by others.

Advocacy In Action continue to challenge all of their partners, learners included.

> We try to do it in a wholly supportive way, but we would hate to think we were exempt from challenge in return, because of some discomfort with our service-user status or power disparity in relation to professionals. Nor, moreover, do we want our learners to lay themselves on the block of their personal experience, only to be humbled, humiliated or silenced as a core requirement of 'learning to work with service users'.

Advocacy In Action view the absence of necessary challenge as the very opposite of good partnership and as an indicator of 'dodgy' power at work. Jackie reflects on Advocacy In Action's feelings, giving her own perspective:

I think it is difficult to challenge service users who are teaching sometimes and I can understand why some are reluctant to do so. Service users and carers often teach using their own experience as a means of starting students on the road to reflecting not only on what has been so generously shared with them, but also about their own personal experiences and how these have shaped who they are. Many things are happening on such occasions. There is a shift in power as service users and carers become the assessors rather than the 'assessed'. They certainly are the ones who are up the front of the classroom and may be asking for reflections that some students find uncomfortable. In a way, what may have been taken for granted as the 'natural' order of things is turned upside down! Where does the identity of being a social worker fit if it is those whom the professional seeks to serve that turn out to be its teachers?

Some students may be scared to challenge for fear of failing. Or they may be trying to understand why the session has such a powerful effect on them. Might students perhaps be shocked to discover that their silence is perceived as 'suspect'?

Sarah and Ed describe experience of a shifting power relationship:

> In early training, Sarah helps Ed learn that he does not need to share everything with people – he is in charge of what people know about him.

Initially the power balance is very much in Sarah's favour. But as Ed comes to start his own business and begins to chair the partnership board, to mix with senior managers and be involved in bigger decisions, 'there is a power shift that we have to learn to manage – to respect that sometimes we cannot tell each other everything – that it is okay for Ed to keep things to himself.'

In the beginning it is important for Ed to realise that, although Sarah has the power of knowledge about him as a social worker employed by the local authority, he, in fact, makes the decisions regarding how much he discloses about himself while they are training together. It is interesting how this power changes, as Ed starts to be privy to information that he cannot always share with Sarah. This turns the situation on its head, potentially causing the partnership to suffer as a result. But the fact that both are able to honestly acknowledge the shift and agree how to deal with it means that in reality, the partnership is strengthened.

Power relationships are complex within The Long Distance Gang, and they travel with the group across to Ireland. Both Julie and Nes meet an occasional problem in resisting the power that others attempt to abdicate to them. At times, for certain travellers, it is easier just to hand over all responsibility for decision-making. So when lapses and slip-ups *do* happen, it won't be the fault of 'the powerless'. There is also a sense that, for some partners, the hassle of always 'doing as you are told', or of dodging and outwitting the power-from-the-top, is less fraught than the risk of reclaiming control. In the pecking orders imposed from *below*, those with *less power*, or with *denied power*, might want people 'above them'. They may feel a need to maintain the security of the known, the painful and the familiar, no matter how oppressive. But Nes and Julie feel compromised by being put in charge.

Abroad in Ireland, however, it is alcohol that creates significant power differences, especially when some partners have to wield responsibility delegated to them by the staff at '32'. In accommodating all the different ways partners choose to define power, there are conflicts with the formal and legal 'well-being' and 'compliance' agendas of the care home.

Nes recalls that 'the only thing that puts some of us in a different place in respect of power is a responsibility for the handling of alcohol and medication – alcohol prominently.' Julie suggests to Nes that people's promise to look after themselves and one another puts into place a shared responsibility that in turn encourages a personal power to self-regulate. Other members all own in hindsight that the respecting of their promise, albeit at times strongly resisted, is a powerful achievement. As Nes summarises, 'where would we be if every urge to drink had been fulfilled? We probably would never have even made it here to Ireland...' So The Long Distance Gang opts for a sharing of responsibility where all partners are accountable for self and others. Ultimately the principle of mutual dependability works very well in re-distributing group power.

> What is very wonderful is just how *responsibly* all partners live up to the control we allocate ourselves. Thus, for example, as we move to self-regulation of alcohol over the week, the constant cravings for 'another drink' which has nipped and niggled from dawn to dusk, calms down

and snoozes, until even the most stalwart of 'topers' are not cracking the first can before mid-day.

For Stephen, the issue of power is crucially important, and he has to honestly acknowledge this to himself to keep the focus on what he is trying to achieve:

The power difference couldn't be bigger. When you decide whether or not a person has mental capacity, it hits you just how vulnerable the person is and how important the decision is. You must acknowledge that power to yourself as it is foolish to pretend that there isn't power in the decision. You have to do your absolute best to empower the service user to ensure the decision is in their best interest. Inherent within the state's functions are responsibilities to provide care, help and services to those in need. This has to be balanced, however, with the responsibility of protecting them from harm, abuse and exploitation from others.

It is important therefore to weigh up in the decision-making process the benefits of one choice over another and consider whether by taking a particular course of action, you are likely to be creating other, sometimes more serious problems. For example, a decision that results in a person being placed into residential care so that their physical safety can be managed more effectively may in some circumstances be at the expense of a person's psychological or mental well-being.

Once a decision has been made, it is important to reflect afterwards and consider to what degree the process has been about empowerment or control.

While June has experienced partnerships when power has been acknowledged and managed, there have been occasions when it has not:

I have to say that it has usually been obvious to me early on when 'acknowledgement' and 'respect' were never going to happen. However, the hardest experience is when you think someone has 'got it' and then through structural or resource pressures they have to draw back on their position. Then tokenism abounds.

It is the research consultant that some OPPS members 'put in charge' and defer to her ideas and suggestions. Although older people *possess* the research and all its processes, they are sometimes unwilling to fully own it — some are even grateful for being 'invited in' instead of recognising that they *are* the research and they *are* the power. Yet, there are within the group retired nursing and social care professionals who have occupied powerful roles in younger days. Does this apparent disenfranchisement have anything to do with the sense of loss of control, value and purpose attached to their ageing?

Mary, as service manager, is also looked up to as in charge. And so, of course, she is! It would be unwise not to recognise the power of the local authority, and we should add that Mary uses it very respectfully and unobtrusively, never crushing others, or taking over.

Julie wonders, however, whether:

> ...people fully grasp the power that service users hold in this research – the power to join in or not to join in, to enable or disable this piece of work that centres so crucially on them – their expertise through experience – and the simple fact that both I and the council *depend* on their involvement.

PAct believes that gratitude and deference hold no place in partnership, outside of the simple human courtesies we all owe one another.

Within *React*, there were power differences between the children, relating to disability. Kara explains how the partners were supported to address these:

> As some of the children taking part in the partnership have a disability, while others do not, there are some differences in power that need to be acknowledged. Some of the pupils have physical disabilities and need supportive equipment to enable them to move around, whereas others are able to move around independently. We work towards empowering the pupils with physical disabilities by enabling them to have control over where and how they are moved. One way in which this happens is through duet movement work. More mobile pupils work in partnership with the less mobile pupils, using their natural movements as a guide for improvisation. For example, when 'Ahmed' uses his wheelchair, partner 'Salim' faces him with his hands next to Ahmed's on the armrests. As other members of the group produce sounds using cause and effect technology and select or play recordings made in previous sessions, Salim moves Ahmed's wheelchair while facing him. The direction and speed of Salim and Ahmed's partner work is controlled in collaboration between the two boys. When Ahmed moves his head to the side, Salim turns left. When Ahmed becomes excited by his favourite music, sounds or lights and claps his hands or bounces up and down, Salim increases the speed of their movement and bobs up and down in time with Ahmed.

Once the pupils learn how to work together in this way, the mobile partners are able to make their own choreographic decisions based on their partner's movement. For example, when 'Haidar' enjoys the strong pulse of the *Red* music, he vocalises by saying 'ouff!' and waves his arms quickly. In response to this, Haidar's partner 'James' practises a spinning jump, which he uses each time Haidar does this. Haidar also enjoys watching his partner jump and often claps and smiles.

This control sharing between the children is an inspiring and creative way of owning differences and enabling children to have fun and learn about mutual power!

Trish finds when she first starts to work with services and the local authority that there are real power differences and ways in which these differences are reinforced. One way that this happens is through language: 'We soon find that professionals have their own secret language. We have to challenge some professionals about this.' Trish begins to unearth the hidden agendas: 'We discover that some other individuals and agencies want to work with us for their own advancement. Part of the learning for us is how to manage these situations and sometimes turn them to our own advantage.'

Difference in status is another way that power differences are reinforced:

> We feel that we have to overcome the barriers between our perceived status as parents and that of professionals. The fact that we are a group has given us the confidence to see ourselves differently. We are the experts on our children.

It is clearly very difficult to be true partners when language and status exclude people and then, in addition, some have motives that are more for their own advancement than anything else. Trish and the other members of APTCOO come to be aware of these issues. They learn about the strength they draw from each other and their combined power to challenge:

> Sometimes it feels that we are being swept along to make decisions by outside influences to fit in with other agendas. There isn't one person making the decisions. We learn together about the times when we are being swept along and we become aware of it and are able to re-focus.

It is APTCOO's awareness of power differences and how they operate that enables parents to deal with them and to challenge the professionals who work in ways that reinforce them.

In summary

All our partnerships convey the necessity of knowing who holds what power at any point in time and how well it is managed.

In a growing space, an honest dialogue about the difference in partners' positions and the power they have as a result will usually be possible.

HOW IS POTENTIAL RECOGNISED AND DEVELOPED IN PARTNERSHIPS?

Everybody has potential which can make its appearance in the most unexpected of situations. Dave reflects on Sean's final Ireland journey as a dying man, and how, 'rather than deplete or lessen Sean, the trip sustains and enriches him'.

Sean shines with energy and power. His beautiful spirit fills the wasted body. He finds his strength to walk a few feet of pasture to the family donkeys in the back field. He strokes them with a glint of wicked humour in his eye: 'take a photo of me here with these three donkeys will ye? And we'll call it the "Four Arvagh Asses!"' Doing his own thing in his own way both enables and *ennobles* Sean. And in assisting this journey, and at this point in time, Julie and Nes both are imbued with a huge sense of being fully '*who* we are meant to be and *where* we are meant to be.'

OPPS researchers grow in confidence and ability through working together in structured and unstructured group activities. And as the months go by, there is no one who is not fully involved in making this important research happen. OPPS members reflect on growing together:

> Every step we take we're getting better and better. I feel ready to take on whatever comes our way. If you had told me three months ago that I would be chairing a meeting, I would have laughed at you, but just look at me now! Fantastic – people grow and learn together – I feel totally joyful and full of energy!

Workers, too, develop: '...it has made me think very differently about life and what I value – think differently about others too. OPPS has made me think more deeply about myself and others.'

React encourages *all* children to recognise their own abilities and those of their peers:

> The pupils are given regular opportunities to perform to one another. This enables them to appreciate each other's work, potential and strengths. Most importantly, the way in which the pupils work together is celebrated and pupils are able to watch video footage of themselves working.

React is a good example of potential being celebrated.

EMAPP also likes to celebrate achievements and to encourage individual members within the group. Jeanette comments: 'I think that people have been encouraged to develop their potential within the group – I certainly feel I have, and that I have been supported by other members to grow.'

The recognition of potential among APTCOO members enables them to move on and to develop further as an organisation:

> People already have skills and we are able to tap into free local training to develop these further. This is a group strategy for those who want to do this. We feed back what we learn to the group and this has increased the overall knowledge of our group.

Reshma and Sherma also find it important to recognise potential in each other and to allow opportunities for this to be developed. Reshma reflects that 'my potential has been recognised early on and encouraged by the fact that Sherma has asked me to deliver the partnership module to PQ students.'

Many of these partnerships suggest it is important not simply to recognise potential in individual members, but to open people up and encourage them to grasp opportunity to build on it.

Advocacy In Action loves to see *possibility* and grow the kinds of spaces where talents and qualities proliferate. They sometimes turn things on their head to do this. So, for example, when a member of the group takes the notion to collect spare change from other people's pockets, they build on her 'finance skills' and encourage her to take charge of the cash box. She guards it like a hawk! Brian too remembers that he is given responsibility when in 2005 he first encounters Advocacy In Action:

> ...me and Stuart go to this meeting at the church place — it's for the homeless and whatever. So Stu and me got beards and scruffy hair and we smell because we got pissed on while we was sleeping on the streets. Anyway, we go in this place looking a right pair of villains (which we're not by the way) and all of a sudden, there's Julie right there with a ticket book and we're being roped into doing the raffle. Well! We could run off with the cash and whatever — but we don't. We can't believe Advocacy In Action wants us with 'em but we join the group anyways. And from here we just get better all the time till we become teachers and lecturers and get a flat and write our own book what people want to buy.

Advocacy In Action unearths 'treasure' in Coventry in 1993, while helping black and Asian parents to stick up for themselves. 'Please work with our sons and daughters too!' begs the parent group. And when young Raja realises he is valued by his new partners, he gains the confidence to challenge his keepers. Raja uses his signs and sounds to tell Advocacy In Action that he believes he is in the wrong place: 'I'm stuck in Special Needs because no one understands my speech or my culture'. Advocacy In Action helps Raja gain assessment from an educational psychologist. Within four months he is doing A-levels at a local college; in four years, he has a first class degree in Mathematics.

Anything is possible if you are willing to dig deep enough to find the seeds of potential in people. This is surely true for Stephen as he works with others:

> Part of the assessment process is to seek the strengths of the person. They can still be involved in the process even if they don't have capacity. They can still be involved in decisions about taking risks. You have to be confident in the decision and so you always have to reflect and not be afraid to ask yourself the question, 'How did you come to that decision?'
>
> In this situation it is about recognising the potential that the person being assessed has to be involved in the process. By doing so, you can give them the opportunity to be a part in the decision-making as far as is possible. Striving to work in this way will make the difference between a practitioner who enables others and one who will not.

PAct members find that everyone's potential is developed through good partnership working, as co-producers or as researchers. Partners feels they have enhanced their expertise and furthermore that they have helped others develop capacity too.

Long Distance Gang members make a list of what skills they have and what skills they would like to gain. When the group test drives the minibus to Matlock, most partners have a go with the video camera. And everyone is an 'expert' on the best motor routes along the west of Ireland's rugged Atlantic coast! Partners recognise that age and circumstances are not a hindrance, and that singly or together people can achieve anything they desire. Previous life skills are not necessarily redundant – within them are elements that can be transferred to the present. And capacity can be built on at any age!

No task is restricted on ability, only by confidence and motivation. But the more trust we place in one another, the greater the enthusiasm and the willingness to try. This trust lays firm roots for the springing up and blossoming of potential. And from the confident completion of small tasks or even small parts of small tasks, people move on to bigger and better – film editing and presentations – and to more satisfying roles and relationships within their personal lives. Everyone comes back from Ireland richer.

Not everyone has such positive experiences of working together, and June comments on this ability of some people to work through barriers as well as the inability of others:

> This really does vary with the understanding of the social factors related to oppression, i.e. personal, structural and cultural barriers. Some allies can work around or beyond these barriers but many cannot. This is becoming increasingly so with the reasons often being attributed to cost pressures, reflecting the current objectives underpinning government strategy and policy.

In summary

Potential is not always recognised within partnerships nor encouraged or developed, as June implies. However, within our partnerships here, there is abundant evidence of how individuals and communities blossom when enabled to reach new horizons. This depends on emancipatory values and ways of working rather than the commodification of partnership within restricted spaces. The challenge here to powerful partners is clear!

There *are* positive ways of working together even when the situations are less than ideal. Find them and use them!

Within a growing space, all partners' potential is recognised and they are given the opportunity to develop and blossom.

Chapter **3**

GREEN SHOOTS

HOW IS TRUST GAINED IN A PARTNERSHIP?

Advocacy In Action (see p.17) wants to have trust in themselves and others, but must learn to temper this trust with experience. Partners remain at all times realistic about what values and other forces are in play and over time they have grown in understanding that what people say and what people do are not necessarily compatible. Situations are not always as they seem on the surface!

> We recognise that in some cases, having a written values statement seems be an end in itself, which serves to relieve people of further responsibility and action. Having said all of this, we remain ever hopeful of 'living the values' and look to each and every partnership we enter into as a real opportunity for learning and growth.

A Place to Call our Own (APTCOO) (see p.18) considers issues of trust within different types of relationships. Trish Green reflects that:

> ...within the group, trust is achieved through shared understanding and commitment to our families. Outside of the core group and working with professionals, we approach people who we know through *first-hand* experience we can trust. Some professionals recommend other professionals who we then include in our group. We find out, through the way people work with us whether they really share our values and are compatible with us.

This seeking out of allies is important to Advocacy In Action and APTCOO to achieve what they want, from a solid base of support and understanding.

Older People's Partnership Services (OPPS) (see p.27) sees that as the research proceeds, professional partners keep their promises to work towards the required changes. Partnership, although sometimes difficult, is proving enjoyable and rewarding. Professional trust is earned through results: 'I feel less afraid of the future...I feel comfortable to share feelings...we work so well together – I go away so fulfilled!' It would be lovely to say that everyone in OPPS is nurtured through the warmth of such trust, but it would not be true. There are some 'outsiders' who are left out in the cold. The two men who come together are barely tolerated by some members; they sit on the edge and do not share in the group work. One is not trusted because of previous experience: 'he brings his own agenda – he only wants to talk about what *he* wants to talk about!' His 'shadow' doesn't speak much English. Silent and neglected, he watches with no apparent understanding. 'He's only come for the fiver' one woman suggests, referring to the expense payment everyone receives. Another woman confides to a friend: 'I'm frightened of him...I don't trust him – it scares me to look at him!' Fear and prejudice are deep-rooted within some older people. And the painful little shoots of mistrust, resistant to reason, push up and push this man out still further.

So pockets of suspicion can be present even where partnerships invest their energy in cultivating trust between people as a green and growing platform for joint action. When people come together from choice, trust doesn't spring up naturally, but when people are placed in partnerships through necessity, then they are all faced with the task of learning to trust others in the partnership. Jeanette reflects that she finds she can trust others in the East Midlands Adults PQ Partnership (EMAPP) (see p.21):

> People within the group have earned trust – I find it very hard to trust anyone and if someone does not fulfil something they say they are going to do I am quite unforgiving about that. So those that I trust have earned my trust through their behaviour – actually doing what they say they will.

Often people do not do what they say they are going to do for a variety of reasons, some within their control and others not. However, it is crucial, if trust is to be won and maintained, that everyone in the partnership considers how they behave towards one another and how to demonstrate their trustworthiness.

Some PAct (Our Promise to Act) (see p.29) members lose trust in partnerships where group decisions and tasks are hi-jacked by individuals without prior consultation, or when different pieces of work are altered or 'edited' without sufficient explanation. PAct also see the goalposts moved round to suit different purposes, so PAct members are quite careful about whom they trust.

Perhaps even more daunting for a partner is when trust is invested in them and expectations are high! This brings a huge responsibility with it. The privilege of being trusted needs to be *repaid* by being as reliable as is humanly possible. Jackie experiences this within the Asperger's Consultation Group (see p.20), where one of the reasons they give for trusting her as facilitator is that her personal experience 'makes it easy to trust her.' Such trust needs to be respected. The group also recognises that '...the partnership sets up an expected trust just by being the type of project it is'. Work with the Asperger's Consultation Group is designed to set up a partnership, so this in itself obviously sets the context for trust. It is so important that ventures purporting to work in true partnership do what they say, and that all involved think through how people work together at every stage. To do otherwise is to devalue partnership working and makes people less likely to trust partners in the future.

Sometimes there are external pressures at work that impose themselves onto a partnership by nature of more distant relationships. Top management, for example, controls through a long-arm hold on Sean's travel plans in the last weeks of his life (see p.25 for more on 'My Final Journey'):

> ...and it becomes essential to challenge these forces and constraints that seek to compromise the freedoms of our partnership. We trust our *own* understandings of our partnership and of our situation in Ireland. This helps us all to feel pain free.

Much of the surplus 'bumf' involves 'responsible management' of alcohol, as defined by policy from the top. But Sean can no longer swallow. The bureaucracy is both superfluous and self-serving. It refuses to see that alcohol abuse is no longer an issue, and insults furthermore Sean's right to make his own decisions, wise or unwise, for even if his capacity to drink is stemmed, cancer has not managed to rob Sean of his full mental capacity.

React (see p.30) openly addresses this issue of trust:

Building trust is an important part of the creative process. Clare and Paul are the creative practitioners employed specifically for the project and therefore did not know any of the pupils prior to this. The pupils from Beaufort School are supported by members of staff whom they know well and with whom have a good existing level of trust. Pupils from Colebourne Primary know each other but do not know any of the other pupils, staff or creative practitioners. This initially creates an 'us and them' type atmosphere. The pupils from Colebourne naturally gravitate towards each other because they feel more comfortable with their familiar peers. Clare addresses this issue through dance warm-ups and games. She encourages all the pupils to perform simple movements and copy one another. The group works in a circle and takes turns to perform their own and each other's movements. No one is left out. Every individual is praised for their contribution. The pupils choreograph simple phrases to accompany their names which showcase their own style and personality. Those who are shy or unsure are encouraged by their peers. The group also tries reciting each other's names and performing their movements with support where necessary. Activities like this are introduced every day and encourage the pupils to think of each other as individuals, rather than two segregated groups from two very different schools. Once the children come to know each other, it is easier to gain trust and begin to work together in pairs and small groups.

React demonstrates how principles of good partnership translate into practice. An environment where trust can develop was created and, when given this opportunity, the children rose to the challenge and began to trust each other and the adults working with them.

Confidence slowly seeds during the year before The Long Distance Gang (see p.24) journey, but it is an early experience away from home, partners believe, that truly earns everyone's trust and unites them as one.

A turning point – Pat on his knees at the water's edge, hands raised in supplication! He has been quite unhappy up to this point, perhaps wishing that he hadn't come? He had a difficult journey, but we don't understand why. He stayed in, was moody the night before. But here, on the wild Atlantic coast, as Pat kneels to the storm, we all get a shared sense beyond words, of something about to happen.

What Pat experiences at this point we will never know. Maybe he comes face to face with his own 'failings', with a vision of all he is not and can never be? But he seems to submit to a giving over to the elements — an absolving — and a freeing of himself from his own shackles. And in this long moment, perhaps Pat realises that he *can* do something with his life, he can *be* and can *do* what he chooses. After some time, Pat rises and comes back to the bus, as double rainbows arch above a grey sea in the brightening sky. The rest of us, standing in the misted rain, shared with Pat in silent communion. There is a release of tension as he returns — no need to talk, no need at all.

Later in the evening Pat begins to laugh, out of the blue — just laughs, laughs and laughs out loud. It is infectious, catches all of us up in spasms, tears running down our cheeks. Pat leads a wild chorus of laughter that enables our collective release, and heralds the complete and joyful dance of our coming together as a group.

Pat has become the physical manifestation of some collective freeing up, a letting go and coming to terms with who we are and where we are going. All those questions of 'Can we do this?' or 'Will we make it?' resolve themselves for the entire group, through Pat's acting out of his own life and of our journey, hands raised up to the sky on the edge of the Atlantic Ocean. And in the replied double rainbow promise of hope and possibility! Accepting that he *is* here and he *is* part of things, Pat trusts that this is a very good space to occupy. Surer, stronger and at peace with his purpose, he becomes a new person. (Two-and-a-half years later, Pat remains a much freer man.)

We are all fully bonded within this. We now understand *how we are in this place together*, that we can travel as one and sort things out as one. There blossoms a spiritual level of trust in the group and of the sustaining power of the group. And when a younger partner has to return to England to face the loss of a child, he is wrapped around with love and support from a combined caring body, rather than from individuals.

We are unafraid to engage with these moments of anguish and difficulty and we are, moreover, able to deal with them together and without the usual recourse to alcohol. In Ireland, in brave and lovely spaces, we are all finding out and perhaps remembering aspects about ourselves, as we retrace past places, faces and dreams and build understandings, hopes and friendships. We have earned a complete belief in how we can open ourselves up, and in what we can set out to try to do together.

In summary

It is important to identify and understand levels of trust and mistrust, and as within The Long Distance Gang and OPPS, to be unafraid of the new territories that laying ourselves open to one another will lead to. It is unrealistic to look for or to expect trust to blossom spontaneously. However, we should open out hearts to its possibility.

In a growing space, people have the opportunity to develop trust in other partners. Where people are invited to trust, this is honoured, and allies are not left disillusioned.

BUILDING ON TRUST TOWARDS CONFIDENCE

Self-assurance doesn't shoot up over night, as Advocacy In Action shares with us:

> In the beginning, members have no confidence. We crawl around the floor. At times, we bang our heads on the wall in frustration. Belonging to Advocacy In Action feels wonderful, desperate, scary and safe, all at the same time! But we place our trust in our group and in one another and this soon starts to seed confidence. In 1990, Advocacy In Action stage the first of many conferences, and people come from all over Britain to join us in speaking out: 'I'm just learning to speak out, but I get there – 'cos you can't stop me!' So affirms Polly to huge cheers and whoops of approval from the audience. All of a single mind!
>
> Polly is followed by Michael (RIP) and then by Kevin, who shakes and stumbles on his speech at first. But the collective approval soon frees up his tongue and the rallying words start to flow out: '...my message to disabled people all over this world is to go out and fight for their rights what they believe in! Thank-you-very-much-from-Kevin!'
>
> Some years later, we are called into the locked male wards of a Midlands hospital. A patient has suffocated in their own vomit, while strapped to the toilet. We are asked to help people speak out for their rights. But one partner tells Kevin: 'you won't get me to speak – it's not like a prison here – you don't get to know the end of your sentence – you speak up for yourself and they just add on more time.'
>
> Later in the day, a purse is missing from one of our bags. 'Call the police *now*' the care staff insist! But Advocacy In Action take it to the patients. We explain we are on benefits and that we need our cash to get the train home. Within half an hour the purse is back with the money

intact. From this point, there is a banishment of fear, a massive solidarity and a freeing up for all of us — human beings first and foremost. People open their hearts to one another and share their stories with a passion.

We put our trust in the group and we are rewarded when the group trusts us and speaks out and when individuals begin to grow the confidence to reclaim control.

Members in other partnerships find acknowledgement in different ways. APTCOO receives a lot of positive feedback from other families, professionals and the local press and communities and this is a validation for them. Trish recounts 'we feel we are going in the right direction to achieve what we have previously learned from other families is needed.'

This trust in mutual achievement together is shared in many of the partnerships, although it is manifested in a variety of ways. Sarah and Ed (see p.22) learn to have confidence in each other and in their own abilities '...by working and socialising together. When we go away for a Train the Trainer's event together it helps us learn about each other's strengths and weaknesses.'

Burgeoning from the success of group work, OPPS members develop their own presentation and training materials to use with councillors, service heads and agencies at a formal launch. Older people define the OPPS benchmarks of support from personal experiences of receiving care. The presenters explain the difference between good and bad help: 'Not good enough for you? Then not good enough for me either!' Personal experience, shared through a trusting partnership, is helping OPPS to work confidently together and to relate to other people within public presentations.

Through relating on a deeply open personal level, while living together in Ireland, Sean, Nes and Julie find ways to share difficult and complex decisions. Sean orchestrates an agreement where from now on *he* will share responsibility with Julie and Nes by self-administering one dose, left as a standby for the small hours. And for the remainder of this stay in Ireland, Sean is completely on top of his pain. In trusting one another at times of crisis, the partners find the confidence to make the right decisions for themselves in Ireland.

Once trust is established, confidence can grow in the partnership's ability and in the ability and values of those within it. This confidence blossoms as a result of time spent working together, and the positive experiences within that. Jeanette, from EMAPP, comments: 'The confidence within the group has grown as the framework progresses through the various cohorts – as we achieve "success" we grow in confidence – as we become more skilled we grow in confidence.' For some, confidence springs directly from the trust people develop in the partnership itself. The process of working as a group gives rise itself to confidence. Asperger's Consultation Group members find that 'working with other people with Asperger's builds confidence.' They encourage each other in what they can achieve. Members describe what builds up trust for them:

> Knowing I can express myself in a safe environment has built my confidence.

> Not feeling like I'm the project and I'm here to be fixed.

> Knowing our skills set will be recognised and that we are trusted.

> Individuals are able to ask for help. The group aims to make sure everyone is included and understands.

These comments demonstrate what can be achieved for individuals in a partnership if trust has been established. The confidence gained inside this partnership is wholly remarkable for a group of people who are not often involved in such a way. It is a true testament to how anyone can really achieve if they are given the chance and are trusted in return for the trust they extend.

The Long Distance Gang try to adhere to the principle of unconditional regard and to the recognition of positives. Some partners have been censured in the past for 'bad habits'. They do not trust that within their own spaces they make their own rules, or that old rules no longer apply. They decide to test it out. But when Pat, Kitty, Joe and Chris stagger back to the bus in Connemara, hanging on to one another for dear life, the other partners only praise that they've stayed together and looked out for one another in their worsened states. There is no mention of 'alcohol abuse', just a warm and caring greeting. (This only *genuinely* works if praise and care are genuine; patronising will fall flat!)

Sean discloses a prison record. Julie shares the violence within her past. Nes laments a lost friend. Kitty describes her orphanage. Chris admits to the troubles in his life. Pat murmurs about betrayal. Over the week in Ireland, many trusting exchanges, no judgements made, no advice given!

People gain trust that they are accepted *as they are* and *for whom they are*. This permits the confidence to adhere to the group's shared boundaries and promises, and also the confidence to step outside them, where there is a need to, in the knowledge that the door will remain open. It is ultimately the sprinklings of trust partners receive from one another that enables, within very arid hearts, a growing self-belief, fragile at first, which promises the fresh green shoots of confidence.

React shows how to nurture in children a growing confidence through technology:

> The pupils have regular chances to perform together and separately. Paul Rogerson uses the *Khoros*® in a variety of ways. *Khoros*® is a series of coloured panels which lock together in different arrangements. The panels are touch-sensitive, they light up and play sounds when touched. Paul asks pupils from Colebourne to record their partners' sounds using a microphone and then helps them to import these onto the *Khoros*®. Pupils then activate their recorded sounds by touching the coloured panels. The pupils are delighted to hear their own sounds recorded and their partners enjoy helping them to record and activate them. This gives everyone confidence in their own abilities as individuals and in their ability to work together.

In summary

None of us start out as experts. We grow confidence in our own abilities from the trust we and others place in our potential to become better than before. All of our partnerships, but in particular the 'bottom-up' stories, testify to the wonderful achievements realised once people and partners start to believe what they are capable of and work towards it.

In a growing space, partners who have experienced such trust and had their potential recognised gain more confidence in themselves and in others within their partnerships.

NEW KNOWLEDGE FROM WITHIN PARTNERSHIPS

The process of working together can enable people to achieve in ways that they might struggle to accomplish on their own. But new ways of working in partnerships can be challenging and anxious times, and so Ed and Sarah work on ways to manage this anxiety and to inform everyone within the partnership of Ed's new business of how people are feeling:

> When Ed starts his business he and the others involved (all of whom have a learning disability) are concerned about what they are letting themselves in for. Everyone (including supporters) makes a one-page profile about who they are and the support they need. Some people also make communication charts – this helps everyone know if someone is having a bad time and what might help them work through it. We sometimes complete learning logs at the end of pieces of work – these help us think about what we may need to change.

Advocacy In Action develops as a business and extends skills within teaching and learning spaces, where students and qualified practitioners, and also service-user and community groups from all over the UK and abroad, engage with the partners to share, discover and understand. People like the group's ways of learning – they say it is fun and non-threatening, while at the same time 'challenging and serious stuff'.

> Everyone tells us that 'the power is shared round better'. It proves that anyone can be a teacher and anyone can be a learner, and that the situation can change in a flash. Advocacy In Action has designed picture cards and exercises to help people learn together; we are still using some from 20 years ago. Our teaching and training has won awards. We have a very hectic schedule. It gives us feelings of the greatest pride that we have got ourselves off the scrap heaps, and made something of ourselves, through our own effort, that others can learn from. It makes us feel very rich indeed.

Both Advocacy In Action and Ed's businesses create ways of working that support all involved and provide good models that others could use or adapt to use in their partnerships.

The OPPS research findings liberate the previously silent voices of older service users in Leicester and release an abundance of knowledge of the lived experiences of receiving care. The results are published and the recommendations lead to an action plan that will inform existing services and help shape new provision.

APTCOO's new knowledge derives from working with new agencies. Trish reflects:

> We value the new knowledge brought by external agencies. The agencies learn a lot from us and so a real knowledge transfer takes place which

enables us to understand each other better. These new relationships also help us to tap into other sources of funding (identifying where funding could be obtained and what language to use in bids).

New knowledge for APTCOO not only enriches the experience of working together, but is also invaluable to further the cause of the charity. This is a common theme. It seems that the bringing of people together in a partnership which is supportive of its members creates a richness of experience for those within which in turn leads to new learning. This is then itself useful in achieving the goals of the partnership.

Reshma Patel and Sherma Patel (see p.31) experience that this new knowledge is the understanding of each other:

> Reshma is able to utilise her own experience and see its relevance to social work theories. She has always worried about social work theories and so relating to them to her own experience helps her gain access to the theories.

The Long Distance Gang's making of a film together push the boundaries of creative knowledge. It is not the first time such an endeavour has been attempted. Julie recalls many films her advocacy group has produced along similar principles. However, this is a far more ambitious venture and everyone learns important truths about working in partnership.

Also liberated within these spaces is knowledge concerning friends and families long lost to certain of the Gang's partners. Tom Sweeney discovers a brother still living and sets off to Connemara in search of him. Brother Martain has understood Tom to be dead. Neither can quite take the knowledge in, as they sit hand in hand on the sofa, rediscovering one another. Sean learns of friends who died in Cavan and cannot believe it. He asks over and over again, 'How's Deborah doing?', receiving the same sad news from every person he asks.

But perhaps the most important knowledge partners take away are the qualities and strengths they learn about themselves and about one another within the group. Particularly relevant are new understandings for Rich, whose previous knowledge of Pat and Sean is turned on its head when he sees them in freer brighter spaces away from the Nottingham homelessness scene. And when one member has to return to England in the face of family tragedy, he learns further how a group can wrap their collective love around someone who is suffering.

In summary

OPPS and Advocacy In Action generate new knowledge and ways of working, while The Long Distance Gang discovers lost knowledge. The levels of self-understanding within all the partnerships enable what Reshma and Sherma describe as new understandings of one another.

Within a growing space, knowledge is shared and learned. Some knowledge comprises new insights into hidden strengths of individuals or of the partnership that can nurture as well as inform.

WHEN PEOPLE FEEL VULNERABLE IN A PARTNERSHIP

Perhaps we should always be a little bit vulnerable. So says Advocacy In Action. People who think they aren't vulnerable may not be in touch with their own feelings – and this is *not* healthy! Advocacy In Action wants to be in touch with how people *feel* within its partnerships and understands that even the best human relationships have the capacity to strip us all to the bone.

Brian longs so much to be loved within the group that he becomes susceptible to the fear of loss. He worries in case people don't like him. He struggles with jealousy when his friends get close to others. Although his drug habit is far behind him, Brian is now 'hooked' on acceptance.

Many in Advocacy In Action are labelled 'vulnerable' because of their conditions and problems. And yes, it is true that living with risk, chaos and distress is not easy. But it is equally true that openness breeds resilience. The two exist side by side. So, if you look at Christine, for example, what do you see – disability? Fragility? Her sweet trusting nature? Look closer! See the strength that resists and forgives the most unforgiving of past events. Now Julie is Christine's carer. Julie is a fighter. 'She's so strong,' people say. But Christine knows an absolute helplessness within Julie at times. Christine recognises, without words, their shared experience as women who survive.

When Advocacy In Action works in spaces with powerful professionals, they want to see the *people* within the roles. Practitioners are encouraged to bring the whole of themselves into the partnership. This can be scary and may make people feel naked and defenceless. But it brings with it the capacity to heal:

Advocacy In Action brings out emotions in me that are hard to cope with. I feel very fragile and raw. I feel so humble. Brian puts out a hand of trust to talk to me face to face. Being able to open up to Brian is a real part of my healing.

I know only too well, as a worker, what it feels like to be humiliated, scared and frightened. Workers are trapped too. We have all this shared experience as survivors. I want to break the trap. I want to influence and promote change. I recognise that we can all of us be more than survivors – we can be fighters.

Back in the beginning of Advocacy In Action, Tessa Harding shares that '…when professionals talk about "vulnerable people" I wonder who the invulnerable ones are!' Advocacy In Action thank Tessa, who has grafted her wisdom onto their understanding. It lives on in all their partnerships.

All within The Long Distance Gang feel vulnerable in Ireland! 'We are in very different spaces, less familiar and safe. We deal with many difficulties, physical, emotional, circumstantial.' Tom, Pat and Julie cannot walk without help. Nes, Rich and Ade are the 'English visitors'. The mental well-being of brother Martain is disordered and precarious. 'We are all in places faced with the unknown and the uncertain, and we have different ways of dealing with this.' Some self-medicate with alcohol to push down the fear. Martain punches Sean and gives him a black eye. Jo goes quiet. Familiar roles are clung to – Julie, the musician, Kitty, the home-maker, Sean, the 'wise-cracker' – all to feel safer and secure. Driver Chris curses every other driver on the road and Nes gets fidgety. 'We do not need to explain it all to one another. As partners, they just understand.' Sean holds his hand out to Martain, Ade offered Chris a cigarette. Everyone accepts Kitty's fussing and puts up with Julie's jigs and reels till their ears pop. In this space, vulnerabilities are accepted and the defences they occasion, tolerated and forgiven:

As a group of people, *we talk about what we are feeling*. This in itself is scary but also healing. Some of us have never had the opportunity to talk in this way before. Others are very used to it. Sharing feelings helps people understand *why* they respond in certain ways, and in this manner gives back some measure of control. Sharing feelings about our partnerships helps everyone to relate to one another with honesty, insight and kindness. The fact that we are all able to feel vulnerable added to the fact that we do all feel vulnerable helps bind us together.

The staff team in England feels cut off. They worry about risk and responsibility and about reprisals. If anything goes amiss in Ireland, they are in the front line of fire. And they cannot even contact the group in Ireland! For manager Dave and his staff team, feelings of defencelessness are linked to a lack of control. Vulnerability, for the workers, is about being out of the picture temporarily.

Understanding *why* people feel vulnerable is very important and helps to put things in perspective.

Although the love and respect between Sean and his partners are a constant support, there are some brutal confrontations during the final journey to Ireland in 2010:

> Sean refuses to quit the pub — and though he cannot swallow it — he fondly strokes and stockpiles the glasses of Guinness and Paddy whisky from well-wishers. Just another song, people urge! And one more round! Julie and Nes are desperate to leave. We are watching Sean round the clock. It is heart-breaking to pull him away and it is also necessary. The morphine is in the cottage and time is running out. When Sean shuts his ears to the demands of pain control, there only remains to accuse him of selfishness. This does the job and we leave. Once home, and medicated, Sean is able to share how secure he feels, surrounded by his booze — even though he cannot swallow it. Sean then admits to his agony. This is not easy for any of us.
>
> Vulnerability is our ally, nevertheless. It enables our completely honest and open engagement, no layers left, stripped to the core. Only now remaining, the need to hold and to be held.

Insight into vulnerability holds equally true for the original parents of APTCOO, as Trish herself relates:

> The nature of the group means that parents carry on being parents of disabled children with all the struggles that this brings and at the same time work in this partnership. It inevitably results in contradictory feelings. We recognise as a group that this happens and individual members are able to have 'time out' and rejoin when they feel able. During this time they still have the support of the group. It doesn't happen very often but it is important that people know they can do this.

Parents also feel vulnerable often when they have a bad experience of other agencies. So it feels threatening to invite some professionals to join the group. It is through discussion and gaining more understanding of where professionals are coming from that people begin to feel less vulnerable.

Trish here focuses on two different causes of vulnerability. First, the stresses and strains involved in being carers, and second, the anxiety caused by bringing in professionals to what has been a fairly safe environment where the parents all trust each other. All the parents understand the first cause of anxiety as they have each experienced it and it has always been this common experience which gives them such unity of purpose. The permission they give to each other to have 'time out' is a natural extension of this common understanding. The second anxiety of professionals entering into the 'safe haven' of shared experience and mutual understanding is a real challenge for APTCOO. Its response of supporting parents to try and understand the professionals – and so see them as less threatening – shows a real willingness to take risks for the eventual benefit of all families of children with disabilities. The decision to understand others rather than see them as an ongoing threat proves a crucial factor for APTCOO's success.

Although individuals seldom publicly own up to any feelings of personal vulnerability, PAct members suspect that many partners, professional and otherwise, experience insecurities within their working alliances. For the majority of individuals, however, this vulnerability is not destructive, and there are good supportive spaces that make the partnerships reasonably safe – certainly not somewhere to flee from when they are feeling opened up and exposed.

Asperger's Consultation Group members also regard the partnership as a safe place and one in which they are understood. One member comments: 'Knowing that I'm understood makes coming to the group easier and if I need to leave it is okay to do so.' This permission from a partnership to 'take time out' when someone is feeling vulnerable also echoes the experience from APTCOO.

Reshma feels the vulnerability created by going outside of a 'comfort zone'. She comments on feeling '…"out of my depth" as I haven't done academic studying for many years'. This is a real worry for Reshma and she needs to address this. The insight she gains from talking to Sherma and to a peer helps her to confront this fear and go on to succeed with her academic writing:

> Reshma needs to go through the process herself of writing the assignment and gaining the self-belief she needs. Reshma and Sherma spend a lot of time discussing the requirements of the assignment and the relevant theories. The partnership needs to have a strong trusting relationship to allow for partners to seek support from outside of it. Reshma accesses peer support and the person is able to encourage Reshma and reassure her that she has the ability to succeed. The willingness of each to allow networks outside of the partnership to access help within the partnership makes it stronger and allows growth to take place.

Vulnerability can spring from within therefore, or can be imposed from the outside.

The restraints of funding always produce uncertainty, and when jobs and services are at risk, the climate for partnership can be overcast. Working partners are unsure at times if they will still have jobs. Will the OPPS research partnership, for example, be compromised in any way? Dark days for us all! Health is also an issue for many members on and off – the itches, twitches and stitches of ageing, and some hospitalisation. Ageing itself makes us all feel exposed at times.

'Mr R', the man nobody speaks to in the OPPS partnership, stops coming. How vulnerable this renders him – being so ignored.

Julie feels defenceless when a core of OPPS members threaten to quit if loud-mouthed 'Mr P' is invited to further meetings. She cannot turn them to any fair compromise and she cannot do without them. If people leave, then the research is finished. Advice to Julie is to put 'Mr P' on hold until the work is out the way and then bring him in again. Principles are compromised by material considerations, and Julie feels treacherous to the bone.

In Advocacy In Action, workers have always been, and remain, unpaid. This principled choice can make them feel very vulnerable. However, lack of money has never stopped the group and has perhaps made Advocacy In Action even more savvy and capable. Julie considers how 'working without funding hones the edge to seize and devour every opportunity to learn with and from one another, as a group and within all our wider partnerships'. The insecurity of little or no funding is not a chosen path for many partnerships, but Advocacy In Action recognises, as a group without too many 'squids', that it has learned instead, to value lived experience and other non-material and non-traditional resources. Julie recognises how 'vulnerability can be turned into strength if viewed and supported in the right way'.

In summary

The awareness and owning of vulnerability is a massive asset within all of the partnerships and alliances – The Long Distance Gang, Advocacy In Action and the travellers along Sean's final journey recognise and protect this. The OPPS partnership is still ambivalent in its handling of its vulnerable places, but is working on these. In general, the less defensive partners become about feelings of vulnerability, the more open they are to learn from it.

Within a growing space, partners will feel vulnerable at different times and in different ways. A growing space will not eradicate feelings of vulnerability but will allow for it to be expressed, respected and owned within the safety of the partnership.

HOW DO PARTNERSHIPS ENSURE THAT EVERYONE IS HEARD?

MacSweeney! MacSweeney! MacSweeney's a c***!

Nes deliberates on the power of film to enable or restrict Long Distance Gang voices:

> I have a feeling that the film and those in the film speak for themselves, so I don't want to say too much. My hope is that it is a documentary in the truest sense, in that it records events but makes no judgement, offers no moral position. As a film-maker there is a sense that what you do sometimes feels like a betrayal of sorts, the more you edit, the more of yourself you are imposing on the end result.

For this reason, the editing of *Arise, You Gallant Sweeneys!* becomes a shared task for everybody.

Julie considers how everyone in the film is very true to themselves in the way they express their lives and feelings:

...nothing tidied up or removed − the language is as rough and ready as the narrative it carries − but this is somehow the ultimate trust we have for one another − that it is okay to just be *who* we are − it would be very, very dishonest if some were to decide how others should be heard.

The Long Distance Gang has to grasp the thorny issue of 'subtitling' − should or should not the film be subtitled? Everyone joins in the debate. If they subtitle *Arise, You Gallant Sweeneys!* will it imply maybe that Irish people can't speak English, or speak it back to front? Will it create a power disparity where some are stepping in to explain on behalf of others? Will it take away from the audience's ability? In the end it is decided to do without.

So the film's voices describe landscapes lost and transformed, and the things that will never alter:

Did ye ever see a 'corncrake'? No? Too many chemicals on the land now − a flightless bird the corncrake − no wings − it just runs along the ground − a bit like me − run to the nearest off-licence − Corncrake Sean!

That's me! I'll never change, I don't want to change.

PAct member Reshma Patel wonders what it takes to really listen and really hear:

Within university partnerships, I recognise that lecturers have good will and want to develop coursework in partnership with people who use partnership and carers. However, it is often the case that they have neither the time nor the resources to invest properly in this activity. And so we all lose out. I feel universities are generally clear that they want long-term achievements and are ready, indeed *required*, to listen to their partners. But this can only be achieved through a fully committed team all willing and able to take responsibility for partnership within their own modules, including holding budgets for their resourcing. There are issues here for internal and external university funding bodies to attend to themselves.

How can partnerships ensure that everyone's voices are heard? Sarah and Ed and the other members of Ed's business really think through ways of making sure that everyone is heard in their meetings:

At the start of all meetings we share a piece of good news − this helps everyone speak early on. Learning logs help to evaluate work. We also always share lunch together before we do formal business. We have graphic agendas for meetings and red cards if people do not understand something.

Advocacy In Action knows there are many ways of speaking out. They learn this in Oxfordshire in 1993. Their partner, Chris Locke, is at this time a local authority manager. He asks them to help develop self-advocacy across the county. Service users become excited at the prospect of having a voice. Most workers want this to happen too. However, there is a thistle to be grasped! The group turn up to one venue for a weekend of 'speaking out'. The service manager greets them with a smirk on his face. He takes them to a room where 20 people sit rocking and screaming.

'Here you go!' he says. 'Make a self-advocacy group out of this lot!'

At this moment, Advocacy In Action are suffused with doubt.

But here is one of the most powerful spaces we have ever created. Hidden voices insist on being heard. When Kevin tells his story and shows a picture of his straitjacket, the three silver-haired women sitting on the floor fasten their arms around themselves and sway back and forth, transported in time to their straitjackets and the long-stay hospital.

Wayne is next to speak. He uses the 'empty chair' to help him. Facing the chair, he begins to 'talk'. A friend knows Wayne's signs and noises and translates for him. A second partner, more confident, is needed to share it with the bigger group. Wayne puts his family on the empty chair. He is talking with his hands, negotiating, begging his parents '…help me – don't hurt me! Don't hit me – help me!'

And the blank-eyed woman, who mutters hexes and spells and plays with a doll throughout, suddenly switches into clear and brutal focus: 'Yes I know the pain of too much love and too much anger in my own family. I had a child once but I lost him when they put me in the hospital. I hope I'd have made a better mother,' before she slips back into her own world once more.

Advocacy In Action partners understand the need to be heard and respect all the ways that people choose to talk to them. We recognise also that they can speak for one another if the need arises. Even the silent person, who sits wordless and watching at the side, embodies for us the right to witness and be witnessed. And when they hear the phrase 'people with listening difficulties', it makes so much sense to us of the behaviours that we sometimes see among our more articulate colleagues. We want to help everyone learn how to *listen from the heart*, in order to grow better partnerships.

The first part of the OPPS meeting is for people to speak about anything they wish. It is very popular, although not everyone gets a word in:

> People are so enthusiastic that there are sometimes two or more conversations tumbling over on another. Group facilitators remind 'noisy' people to partner up with quieter members and bring them in. Someone needs to help 'Mrs P', whose confidence is a little low. But then the chatter builds up again, so 'Mrs P' sits back and just smiles. During the more structured parts of the meeting, Julie ensures that people work in supportive twos and threes so that everyone has their say. But the opening space is a free for all and is less considerate at times.

For APTCOO, making sure everyone's voice is heard becomes more of a challenge as the project grows. Trish reflects back on what is going on at this time:

> Two elements developed — the support side and the management committee. The support side feeds into the committee, so for those who don't want to be part of the more formal side, they can still have a voice. All committee meetings are open, so anyone can come along and say what they want. We now employ community workers and they are another link to the community and so even more voices are heard. We have formal consultation processes through formal and informal means so we feel that we have a fairly accurate idea of how other families in the community are feeling and we are now in a position where we are able to represent them.

EMAPP have a service-user co-chair, Kevin Chettle, who always starts by asking that people share something about themselves, and this gives the meetings a warm and far less formal beginning. Larissa Barker, a Stakeholder Board member, summarises what she feels has enabled everyone to have a say in the meetings: '...a good chair person — recognising and acknowledging contributions'. Jeanette also recognises that it is the way that meetings are run that enables people to be heard: '...the meetings [help] — asking everyone if they have anything more to add helps'. The pace of the meetings is therefore important, and ensuring that people can reflect on what is being discussed and have a chance to say more if they want to.

PAct members experience difficulties in ensuring that everyone gets a chance to speak in professional forums. This slows things to the frustration of some members. Yet there are also the uncomfortable silences filled to bursting with all that remains *unsaid.*

The common thread between these partnerships and how they try to ensure everyone's voice is heard is that they think about it and then take creative, respectful and practical steps to ensure that everyone gets their say. Where, for whatever reason it does not happen, then partners need to take responsibility for and learn from this.

In summary

The smallest voices insist on a hearing and within the respectful partnerships they resonate loud and clear, as Advocacy In Action demonstrates. OPPS and PAct show, however, that the necessary human respect to enable this sometimes needs a little nurturing.

In a growing space, partners have the freedom to express what is important to them in all aspects of themselves – and this is not just listened to, but heard. A growing space encourages and allows this to happen.

AS PARTNERSHIPS BECOME ESTABLISHED, WHAT HELPS AND WHAT HINDERS?

Julie sees how power bounces backwards and forwards between individuals in Advocacy In Action. The conventions of who is supposed to be powerful or powerless are often challenged by the sort of group interactions, where articulate women occupy most of the space and men are reduced to passive partners, or knowledgeable workers with a disability bully less well informed colleagues for using the 'wrong words':

> ...the pain of challenge does not diminish as we grow. And issues of power are alive and thriving – the old standards and some newer varieties – but we try to keep it all in the open and managed through supportive discussion and positive example.

People begin to see that *poor challenge of unfair practice* can itself be an abuse of power. Members recognise a need to develop the confidence and understandings that help them see true humanity in one another.

Different people joining the group over time assist this good growth. Advocacy In Action is slowly getting there. The Long Distance Gang is also on the move.

> And it is specifically the removal of labels — 'drinker', 'worker', 'care needs', 'professional', 'hostel-dweller' — together with their underlying assumptions, that enables the sharing which binds us all so intrinsically together as mutual supporters, mutual discoverers, mutual storytellers and mutual creators.

It is also, Dave, Julie and Nes suggest, the unanticipated emergence of sets of *unusual or difficult circumstances* that test the partnership, develop it, and through which the new growth is detected. Such challenging situations occur on a daily basis, while the group is away in Ireland. Nes and Julie recall:

> ...a sense in which we are all in this together — even when we're scrapping! An understanding that ultimately we are on one another's side, and that challenging each other brings us closer when we are sorting out our differences — we are people who challenge because we *care!*

The importance of the group promise helps them to resolve unanticipated dilemmas. When Pat dives into the drinks crate on a bus ride from Clifden, partners question him. Later, when drinks are handed around to others, Pat declares he has already had his. Although angry, Pat sees the bigger necessity to share and he goes without.

Joe challenges Julie when she refuses to let him buy her an Irish feadog (whistle):

> We agreed to give one another respect — yet now you're rebuffing my little token? What makes you feel yourself entitled to refuse my respect of buying you a gift?

Sean declines to get on the return bus from his birth town of Arvagh. He has decided that he wants to stay on in Ireland and not go home to Nottingham. He turns his back on the group and walks away. It is Julie who chases after him, to remind Sean of the promise between individuals to look after one another, signed up to by one and all. Sean hesitates and stops. He takes his promise out of his jacket pocket and reads it. He gives a deep, deep sigh, shrugs his shoulders, pulls Julie into a rough bear hug, and returns back to the group. It is Sean's own signed statement that pulls him back in.

As individuals, the partners tug in many different directions, but as The Long Distance Gang, they choose to remain united in path and purpose. It is this signed-up-to commitment to 'togetherness' that is especially helpful while they are away. But the new situations that occur on a daily basis in Ireland are less frequent once individuals return to Nottingham and to the old routines and roles. Finding opportunities to develop themselves, outside the constraints of daily lives, proves to be a tall order.

Helpful contributions from workers are significant to the OPPS partnership well-being. Support worker Reshma Patel offers warmth and safety. The 'organic' involvement of two council officers becomes crucial. It is Jullette, the reviewing officer, who is able to persuade older care clients to agree to be interviewed, while team assistant Amita holds all the strands together and magically weaves them into interview partnerships. This enables OPPS to progress and get results in on time.

Sean, Nes and Julie find it helpful to share thoughts and feelings while in Ireland. Partnership is their strength, and on return to Nottingham, it inspires and welcomes back in to it all the staff and residents of '32'. But someone is missing! Tom Coffey, now dead, is back for burial in Ballyhadreen − home at last! A quick end, Tom dies in hospital on the day of his admission. No time for plans or final wishes, the family decides. And Sean, Julie and Nes all worry whether Tom will rest easy in Ireland. But now it is time to talk through Sean's end-of-life decisions. This conversation is difficult for partners. Sean puts it off day after day. *Honest dialogue* helps resolve issues and bring some peace. Honesty is truly at the core of all we do.

How people work together in partnerships is crucial. Although the Asperger's Consultation Group is still a fairly young partnership and have been meeting together for a year at the time of writing, they are able to reflect on what they believe will help them work effectively together in the future:

> We do not need to agree with each other to make a pleasant experience. There has been no need for confrontation as different experiences and opinions are respected. Different opinions and experiences form the foundations and building blocks for helpful discussions.

Experiences of PAct members within formal research partnerships suggest that there are always different agendas around from the outset, which can hinder the best of partnership working as they are not always explicit or compatible. For some people personal commitment conflicts with organisational values and creates tensions within university processes and structures. Additionally, the legal 'ethics stuff' absolutely mires people down. PAct members sometimes but not always manage to resolve issues of intellectual property and shared ownership. On top of all this, contractual arrangements between various partners can be somewhat vague.

However, there are plusses too. Where partners work well together, they can come up with inspiring and relevant results. Such partnerships can also form a good support network for one another and are a formidable force of solidarity and/or challenge when they need to be.

A much younger partnership sets about ensuring that the children involved have a positive experience of the activities and of working together. Kara, from *React*, explains how this is achieved:

> As the partnership involves groups of pupils who were not familiar with each other, a variety of team building and 'getting to know each other' exercises are introduced from the outset. At the beginning of the project, the pupils from Colebourne Primary School are slightly nervous about coming to the sessions and, when we collect them from their classes, they come with an air of cautiousness. Working with new adults, and with peers with disabilities, is certainly contributing to this nervousness. After all, the pupils had been chosen as a result of their attitudes towards their peers from Beaufort School. When pupils become more comfortable around one another and their environment, all of them begin to see the project in a new light. Children become very keen and jump up excitedly as soon as it is time for the next session. They express their enjoyment at the end of sessions by constantly asking when they can come back and whom they will be working with next. However, this new-found enthusiasm also leads to some inappropriate behaviour. For example, they will sometimes not pay attention when it is another's turn to perform. Where pupils learn outside of the classroom environment, it can be difficult to maintain good behaviour – the pupils are away from their usual class teacher, support staff and classroom rules. When incidents such as these occur, we adopt the

approach of reminding pupils of the mutual respect we have gained. It is difficult to find an approach to these behaviours that does not curb their enthusiasm; after all, we know that they are merely having fun and therefore getting excited. This does occasionally become a hindrance to the process, but we are usually able to manage the pupils' behaviour without having to use sanctions or 'tell them off'.

EMAPP also highlights positives that can lead to a hindrance. This is a partnership with well-established and strong relationships within it, but members reflect on how this can lead to difficulties. Jeanette recognises that:

> ...what has helped is the development of strong trust and relationships – this may also hinder as not everyone may feel included in those relationships – however, I have never felt that.

Larissa also sees the danger of familiarity:

> A hindrance can be getting too complacent with each other – and also assuming that some tasks can't be done as they have been tried before and not succeeded.

Julie and Kevin both worry when EMAPP partnerships become too cosy:

> ...never, never sit back and think everything in the garden is fine – over-familiarity breeds resistance – it encourages collusions to tangle and snare us up.

When clusters of individuals within any partnership have more to do with each other and so know one another better, there is a danger that others may feel excluded. This may then discourage the 'less involved' from trying to take part in certain activities.

Sarah and Ed also struggle with people assuming that Ed, and only Ed, can do particular pieces of work, rather than employing other service users 'Ed becomes seen as *the* person to ask for user involvement by staff in Nottinghamshire – something he works hard to change so that others get a chance'. Where achievement in a partnership leads to the mindset that people involved in the successful work should always be the ones to do this, it becomes self-perpetuating. The few people become even more successful at working together while others merely stand aside or show reluctance to extend chances to others.

Trish also cites how positives themselves can give rise to hindrances. APTCOO has grown in strength over the years, and Trish attributes this to: 'trust in the value of what families say and trust gained through positive experience of working with some professionals'. Members in the partnership have also been able to: 'stick to our core values, not be afraid to examine what we are doing, and see if it is still a positive force for the families'. Trish is reassured that: 'APTCOO has grown organically and it feels like everything is led by the parents and their needs, so this reassures us about its relevance'. These positives also lead to hindrances, however, when:

> ...other agencies expect us to do something which we have no funding for – where we have become by default the service that will support children and families that do not meet the eligibility criteria of any other agency. This becomes a pressure – as we are then these families' only means of support. We also come to be regarded as the service that can fill any gap in services – but with over four hundred families that we know, it is impossible to support them all, for example, at every multiagency meeting. There is a danger that we will lose our radical identity by becoming just another service. We become aware that we have to challenge ourselves and others to keep our focus and stay true to our original purpose and vision. However, the position we have gained has enabled us to challenge services when this is needed. Some things have changed as a result of our challenges.

APTCOO's experience is remarkably similar to that of Advocacy In Action, which finds that within two years of inception, it has fast become a victim of its own success. Advocacy In Action members recall:

> ...all of a sudden everyone wants a piece of us – just because we won a few awards – and because folk do well in the Advocacy In Action what don't do well in day centres and 'projects'. Kevin's pictures are selling like hot cakes and the women's group has been on telly – we even got these student nurses on 'replacement'! We tell 'em what words to use and how they got to treat us.

Before Advocacy In Action realise what is happening, every minute of every day is taken up. People come to visit from all over England and abroad. There are bags of post to respond to. Local and national committees court their involvement. Training diaries are booked solid – sometimes they have to send out two or three teams. Every conference wants their name on its speakers list. They are even starting to write articles and book chapters!

Kevin and Pauline complain:

> ...folk are landing here from all over the place — social workers chuck 'em our way — they call it 'referral' — we call it 'dumping'...some of 'em say they don't want to be here — it's put on their timetable — Advocacy In Action — Wednesday afternoons (if you want it or not!).

Julie remembers:

> ...and then it all gets just too much. Advocacy In Action is so big it starts to feel like a day centre. We lose sight of ourselves and our vision. We stop growing good ideas and in their place we grow resentments. We are tired and we are trapped — there is no breathing space, no brightness to turn to. Our lovely energy just shrivels up and dies.

In summary

It is salutary and wise to recognise that what hinders and helps can stem from the same source. Advocacy In Action learn from this experience that big is not always good in partnerships, and that scaling down, stepping back or opting out are not necessarily signs of failure.

That strengths can mutate to weaknesses is an important lesson for partnerships. But as APTCOO and Advocacy In Action both demonstrate, self-awareness can guard against the signs of decay and enable people to act to avoid the dangers. Partners should never stop taking stock of where they are. If complacency is avoided and people continue to challenge themselves, their partnerships will grow and develop.

A growing space is aware of when situations are on the move. It is sensitive and responsive to changes within and around it.

SIGNS OF SICKNESS AND HEALTH

Dare we seek for health in the last stages of dying? Sean has refused most nutriment, but is still trying and failing to swallow warm water with a splash of booze in it. So what is health to Sean himself? We believe that *being in charge to the end* is the core of Sean's well-being as he lets go of his life. And this is the crux and rationale of the partnership. In defending Sean's *right to control*, as allies we challenge the signs of sickness — the self-serving sympathy, the taking over by others, the 'over-medicalisation' of Sean's death — and we do not allow ourselves to be infected.

Advocacy In Action hasn't always been good at recognising when it is getting poorly!

> We are too busy and too disorganised in the beginning. So when we begin to burn out, we ignore the warning signs. And we lose a good co-worker in 1993 when she says that she just cannot take it anymore and wants out. Twenty years later, people take time off when they need to. The door is always open — either way.

So partnerships can be sick too. All of the partnerships have a regular health check. Where they are found to be stagnant or moulding over, Advocacy In Action try to sort them out, and if all else fails, they uproot themselves and move off to greener opportunities.

> In the late 1990s, Advocacy In Action co-workers are on so many boards and forums that they can hardly think straight.
>
> The sorts of questions we then ask ourselves are, 'Who are we here for?', 'What purpose does it serve?' and, importantly, 'What has changed because of our involvement?' This helps us see whether the partnership is alive and growing.

While the close bonds between the core members of OPPS are definitely helpful, the group is hindered by previous 'history' between certain individuals and by some poor attitudes towards those faces that 'don't fit.' And there are new little prickles, as 'expert elders' wrestle with the problems of remaining open to newer, less-experienced members whom it is declared will 'lower' the group's effectiveness and reputation.

The OPPS partnership is still young and fragile in its confidence and self-belief. Growing ownership of OPPS has been both a hindrance and a help — good when people put it to good use in the partnership, and disappointing when a few try to take over and exclude others!

Some older members of OPPS never quite get over the awe of professional partners and for some, deference slips dangerously close to subjection at times. Eye contact swerves towards the manager at the door or the councillor sat at the head of table. This is not to say that local authority partners are not deserving of some admiration. The daring confidence of the service director partner, Mary, for instance, proves very useful in helping negotiate the sort of contract that leaves the legal eagles of the council flapping up and down in alarm and OPPS members jumping for joy.

However, all thorny problems in reaching shared ownership of research findings have now been grasped and dealt with. And a disparity between the early research aims and what the council presently want delivering has been resolved. OPPS members feel that the complete independence and commitment of Julie, the consultant, has enabled them to retain their original research vision and values, although this is buttressed by great flexibility and commitment from council officers and leaders. Each partner is helping in their own way. There is a real culture of openness and sharing.

PAct members, on the other hand, have experiences of shared tasks and rewards being 'nabbed' by individuals, and instead of openness and transparency, there is at times secrecy. And also split allegiances! Often partnership appears to be about meeting the aims of others rather than truly shared activities. Interestingly, members feel that some of these alliances have learned through their mistakes, becoming strong and durable as a result of dealing with inner blight, and have not only blossomed healthily towards the end but have produced some lovely and sustainable off-shoots, including strong working relationships. But only after lots of sustained effort!

PAct member Reshma Patel reflects on her experiences of unhealthy partnerships:

> ...my general feelings about partnership are as follows. I have worked with many different organisations both nationally and locally and in most cases my experiences remain the same. When using the term partnership it is important to recognise exactly what each stakeholder is gaining and risking.
>
> Organisations invite me, in the name of 'partnership', to help *them* achieve *their* aims and objectives. I make choices to accept or decline the offer. If I join in, I then have another set of choices to make – and again it's entirely up to me. It is up to me whether or not I decide to go along with them at this stage – not challenging their misappropriation of the P-word, or whether alternatively, I resolve to work with them to help them realise that partnership is about working *together* and sharing the *same* aims and objectives.

However, Reshma recognises that sicknesses *can* be remedied:

I do have experience of where I have been able to take working with a university in an initially tokenistic gesture and turn it into true partnership. The strategies employed and lessons learned in this experience have been very useful to transfer to my current work with local authorities, where a recent example for me of positive change has begun with a local authority seeking a public stakeholder group. They 'seed' their partnership by holding a series of events that are more like consultation exercises of the well-trodden 'our-plans-your-views' route. But through the positive commitment of those of us who attend these early meetings, we succeed in getting them to recognise *how* we expect them to work in real partnership with us. The journey has been long, filled with staff changes and different agendas. However, more recently, we are beginning to see the green shoots of a flourishing *mutual relationship* where our formal partners recognise the benefits of sharing confidential policies with the people who can comment on them from the inside knowledge of their own lived experiences.

In any partnership a good indicator that it is a healthy partnership is that people are free to speak out and express their opinions. However, there may be times when people just don't feel able to.

In EMAPP, every effort is made to give people the opportunity to say what they think, but Mick and Jeanette both question whether this is always the case for everyone. Mick comments:

> ...interesting one! I'm sure there have been some occasions when people haven't felt able to speak out – even though communication regarding agreements and developments have been consistently shared with all partners through appropriate formats to ensure opportunities were available to give opinions.

Jeanette shares the uncertainty: 'I am not sure – I hope everyone now feels able to speak out.' EMAPP, a partnership where people are encouraged to speak out and everyone listens to each other with respect, suspects nevertheless that some just don't! Ed and Sarah also recognise where individuals have initial reluctance:

> ...at first people are scared to speak out – but over time people get more confidence – people have seen Ed as their leader – if Ed says 'okay' there's been a tendency for others to just say 'yes' – but over time people are starting to question Ed's ideas and sometimes they make Ed think again.

Ed has been working with a group of adults with a learning disability. They have not been in the position of working in a business before and so they all look to Eddie. This can happen in any partnership where there is a strong leader and other people are less experienced. The sign of health in this partnership is that people are able to gain confidence in the group and move on to a position where they feel able to say what they think.

Trish describes how this growing in confidence to speak out has developed in APTCOO:

> As the project grows, different professionals join the management committee, some who are quite senior in their organisations. This means that initially the parents on the committee don't understand the language used about government *initiatives* and *strategies* and this knocks their confidence a bit. After a while, the use of jargon language is challenged and the professionals involved are happy to explain once they realise their language is excluding people. There is also an initial perception by the parents that they are being judged on their ability to care for their disabled child. Although they are providing very good care for their child, they feel that they are not on an equal power level. They feel that they are being looked down on, although this isn't actually the case. Some professionals acknowledge at the beginning that the parents are the experts in their children, whereas others realise this as they work with the group and as relationships within the group grow.
>
> As the group develops, a two-way learning process takes place where parents learn how to think more strategically and the professionals learn how to work in partnership with parents. Learning takes place about the purpose of the committee meetings. Sometimes parents might need to talk about the challenges they face as parents, but it is agreed among the parents that emotional support happens before or after the meeting – not during it. Together we find a form of meeting that is neither too formal nor too informal and a place where parents do not offload their frustrations on professionals at the meetings.

There are additional issues to address in this partnership from the bringing together of parents and professionals. APTCOO has to address this issue directly as the inclusion of professionals could derail the partnership due to misunderstandings on both sides.

Signs of sickness are detected in and around The Long Distance Gang partnership – residents who feel left out or ignored or practitioners whose power is threatened. However, perhaps the biggest danger is the bureaucracy of institutional care practices. Much of social care policy and provision appears to promote well-being, only to then act against it! Health and safety, protection of the 'vulnerable', risk management, all are now *ends* instead of *means*, in place to protect, to encourage freedom, but with such frightening power to inhibit and restrain! So, when safeguarding smothers creativity and growth, and risk management strangles possibility and opportunity, the signals of well-being mutate into genuine indications of sickness.

Although there are occasional minor symptoms on the ground at '32', the mortal signs are to be found in the higher and distant branches of senior management and policy-making. However, the involvement of advocacy volunteers helps keep the partnership person-centred and practical.

It has to be said that the time and effort invested into Long Distance Gang shared process and values at the beginning help reduce the distances that bureaucracy and task-based practice might have otherwise created among the partners. Quite crucially there is no specific pressure for things to happen unless people agree for them to – this partnership is all about the forming of bonds. Eventual success is in its mutual ownership. Dave at '32' detects signs of health where: 'staff engage with residents in a broad and open way – genuine interaction around shared experiences – joint purpose and ambition'. The staff team absorbs the positive values into the '32' work ethos. They become very protective of, and even begin to champion, the novel ways of working. A budding confidence spreads across the care home as workers start to see, in themselves and in the men they support, new, fresh growth.

Nes and Julie see the health of this partnership:

> ...in the creation of a communal space that wasn't there before – where people gather as 'equals' – or at least on an equal footing – and in the idea of *dialogue* in all its forms, and in the most genuine of ways, as a mutual transferring of knowledge, camaraderie and skills.

In summary

Partnerships experience split allegiances, secrecy, competitiveness versus cooperation, transparency and mutual support; self-confidence and positivity versus negativity and self-doubt; and good power sharing versus unhealthy power games.

Even within a growing space, partners can feel uncertain and disempowered. Complacency must not allow poor practice to creep in, and vigilance is required to ensure the space is kept as a growing space and does not become restricted.

FEELING VALUED, LISTENED TO AND INVOLVED

For Long Distance Gang member Tom Coffey, who never makes the trip to Ireland, his place in the film is firmly secured through the immortal stories of *The Three Hand Rammers Down the Trench* and *Mary Murphy and the Two Burned Suits.*

Tom is filmed in his room, strong cider to hand, as he 'tells all to the camera' in conspiratorial manner, averring to watchers that 'every word is the truth!'

The Long Distance Gang invites other residents and volunteers to become involved in getting the film ready for showing. Everyone chucks in ideas for venues and invite lists. The partnership broadens as more musicians come on board to enhance the backing track. It is the original partners, however, who decide that the first screening will be in the grounds of their own home.

A balmy July evening alive with activity! There is soup to be stirred and seating to be arranged. Guests start to arrive. Sean and Julie stand together at the front to announce the film programme. Long Distance Gang members are all involved, chatting to dignitaries and friends and welcoming others into what is very much *their space*. And from this first triumphant showing, partners can see they have a 'hit' on their hands. Grins spread across faces and cans are raised in salute – 'Here's to Us – We Did It!'

Following the success of its premiere, *Arise, You Gallant Sweeneys!* draws more and more people into The Long Distance Gang partnership. There are local writers and cinema directors hoping to 'take it places'. Sniffing a winner, housing, health and local community organisers also want in. It is quite a challenge to ensure that the focus always remains *with* and *on* The Long Distance Gang.

Ed tries to pay particular attention to making people feel welcome and listened to when he set up his training company:

> We start each meeting informally with food. We do a round of good news. But sometimes when people find a topic difficult and do not understand it, we have to move on – it is hard to go at everyone's pace and get the company off the ground and at times people feel angry and let down – we have had to work through this.

'My whirlwind Gypsy Gaynor!' Sean's daughter flurries back into his life. Reunited over the past three years, visits have been sporadic but, as Sean worsens, Gaynor realises she is going to lose him. Julie telephones his sisters, Maureen and Kathleen, to tell them time is running out. All these 'new partners' are part of Sean's past, but they have the inexorable right to be involved in his present. It is essential that everyone is heard. But there is much emotion in the air, as past pains spring up to mingle with the new.

Members of PAct question whether partnerships look after themselves as well as they might, and recognise that there is often not the time to reflect or celebrate until the task is over. PAct members feel it is important to understand what has helped or acted against good involvement.

Older interviewees reflect on how well they are helped to join in the OPPS research:

> …you reassure me that it won't come back on me (what you say today might come and bite you tomorrow!). It's nice to know there are people who are interested in us. People think that just because you're getting on in years, then you got no sense at all, you got no feeling, no life, you don't want to know anything. I hope that speaking to you will show everyone a different side to us.

Asking people's feedback, opinions and feelings is a way of helping involve them, as the older people of OPPS here demonstrate. In EMAPP, Mick comments that 'great efforts are made to ensure welcomes are extended and opportunities provided at forums via communication in order for people to feel able to participate.' The programme leader makes sure that new people who are going to work with the university are invited to come and meet her and colleagues as part of their induction in an attempt to get to know people and help them to understand the importance of the partnership working aspect of the programme.

In summary

The languages of involvement are many – emotional, raw, silent and unspoken, in addition to more conventional terms of engagement. Sub-texts may operate independently or be intertwined with formal agendas and processes.

In a growing space, efforts are made to make all participants feel valued, heard and involved. Thought and discussion are dedicated to processes of inclusion and ensuring that no one feels left out, isolated or ignored.

WHO OWNS THE PARTNERSHIP?

People take more pride in something if they 'own' it. This is also true of partnerships. Kara showed this within *React*, through children's responses when they are proud of what they have achieved together:

> Everyone in the partnership is equally valued and has ownership over its direction. All the pupils show pride and enjoyment in their work. As part of our project, pupils are able to perform their final piece to both of their schools, in another school and at Birmingham Town Hall. The performance space is created using sounds and projections of the pupils' work which are triggered live on stage using *Khoros®* and *Soundbeam®* (a movement-sensitive device which can be used to create sounds or to trigger images and videos). Several pupils love their performance space so much that it is difficult to get them off the stage! There are some incidents where a pupil who should not be performing in a particular sequence wanders happily onto the stage or remains on after their performance because they are enjoying the space so much. Often these pupils remain there – they have a right to own the performance and decide upon its direction. Partner work is at the centre of every performance. Every pupil has a partner who works equally with them and every pair has an equal chance to perform. The final piece is split into four smaller performances with a colour theme. The colour themes, videos, images and sounds match the movement styles of the performers in it. Often partners congratulate one another after their performances or sit and socialise together when they are off stage.

Now that The Long Distance Gang has a film to its credit, the partners have to parry takeover bids to retain ownership of the film and of all the processes that have united them in making it to Ireland – and making it to the Nottingham Broadway Cinema!

At one screening, Irish embassy officials are invited. Irish partners are over the moon. Everyone dresses up for the occasion and arrives at the venue in good time to meet and greet. However, The Long Distance Gang is sidelined as theatre directors and local Irish leaders take over the introductions. And while at the finger buffet, these 'big-wigs' feed on their seafood and their self-regard, the group's older men and their allies simply watch from the wings. Julie recalls:

> ...a complete failure and embarrassment as people try to patronise us with a few bland tributes – the men just shut up and switch off – and then it strikes me that these other people neither understand who we are and what we are, nor do they want to know – it is *they* who are out of place in our company.

And there are others who, if unable to control, would try to compromise the group's integrity. Julie and Nes hear murmurings about 'permissions', 'waivers' and 'consents', which not only serve to render some older partners as 'without capacity' and 'vulnerable people' but also seek to encourage them to sign away some very significant rights. Nes deliberates:

> ...it's a turning on its head of its purpose – how can you enter into something honestly and mutually if you have given away ownership of it before the process is even begun? Why should you sign away what is yours?

At work here is a dismissal of the *shared ownership* that *everyone* has over the film rights. Giving *permission* for material about you to be used implies the film must belong to someone else and that it is *they, not you* who makes decisions and profits from them. But in The Long Distance Gang spaces everyone makes the decisions, everyone does the work, everyone owns the partnership and everyone reaps the profits!

Good shared ownership exists in OPPS between Leicester City Council and the older community group. Both require the other to fulfil the research. OPPS needs the backing of its powerful partner, while the Council depends on the grass-roots knowledge and opinion unlocked by its older allies. This growth through mutual dependency is a true symbiosis.

The quality of the EMAPP course has often been attributed (by its programme leader) to the fact that everyone has been involved in developing it together, so all partners feel like it is their programme. Mick comments that 'the partnership has received a consistent message from members (some who have come and gone) of feeling able to undertake a genuine and effective role within the partnership.' However, Jeanette cautions that this may be not true for all: 'This is a difficult point – I have at times felt some people do not share the ownership as much as others and expect more from some people than others. I have voiced this.' PAct associates recognise that ownership within formal alliances is often skewed by professional corporate aspirations. Julie recalls an academic research partnership where 'as a corporate body, the university requirements regarding demonstrating research outputs do not always fit with the group's equality agenda.' There are, for PAct, unresolved issues around who owns research and its findings within formal partnerships. The collaborative research model might suggest a shared ownership but it is often the university, organisation or authority that wants legal possession.

Gina recalls an example of poor practice where a digital report records interviews with a number of service users and carers, none of whom get mentioned in the credits. Julie remembers a similar situation some years previously where a group of black and Asian parents and carers physically lock up the 500 videos produced by their local authority until they are guaranteed a response to issues they have raised!

Nevertheless PAct do have some good examples of truly shared ownership with universities and local authorities. OPPS is one such success. And the digital communities created by the University of Bradford with Advocacy In Action and the University of Central Lancashire (UCLAN) are mutually owned by all of the participants.

Ed wants to be sure that his training company is owned by all the members, but he finds this difficult to achieve:

> ...we are still working towards this – we want more directors with a learning disability but the benefit system makes this difficult – everyone has an equal vote on all major decisions...but at present...Ed is the only director with a learning disability.

'When is the best time to bring in the service users?' organisations have asked over the years. Advocacy In Action respond to say 'if we are not there at the beginning we may never be more than invited guests at the party!' Sharing power also proves a difficult issue for Stephen when assessing people:

To the best of your ability you take all steps possible to help them make the decision for themselves. If this is not possible, the decision must be in their best interest. This can result in the decision being about them but it is not always about what they want.

In living every moment of his final weeks, Sean truly *becomes* his own person and the most powerful person in the partnership. It is the power of facing his death and his dying and making it his own.

When Sean enters a hospice, for 'assessment', someone at '32' lets it slip he won't be coming out. Julie is desperate. Sean hates the hospice. Julie interprets for Sean and writes up his wishes. She leaves his wishes in his hand in the ward and also takes them with her back to '32', ready to do battle if necessary. Julie reminds staff of their *person-centred* ethos. 'What is more central,' she asks of them, 'than being able to choose where you live and die?'

There is resistance from some workers – 'We don't do palliative care – we're not geared up for it!' 'Well get into gear!' says Julie, on behalf of Sean. Dave agrees with Julie and seeks the funding. Dave recognises what is required, by Sean and by the staff team, and he puts it straight into place. Sean comes home to an adapted room and to the Crossroads carers who will meet his extra needs. Dave reflects how 'Sometimes night staff can simply sit with Sean and comfort him.'

The Long Distance Gang enjoy their fags and cans in Sean's room and Sean enjoys watching them. When Julie visits the day before the end, he struggles in vain to raise himself from his chair. 'I need to make ye a cup of tea,' he gasps. Then Sean tells her off for being late! The last word, as usual!

Collaboration is hard at work in these few final days, and powerful too! The determination and daring of every partner manages to resist the 'standardise, sanitise and hospitalise' regime of resource-keepers and 'risk avoiders'. Sean's room becomes the powerhouse – friends and allies united by his will.

'All of this is permitted, indeed directed,' Nes reflects, 'by Sean's final wish to die how he wants – in peace and dignity, in *his* place of choice, surrounded by his family and friends.'

In summary

Ownership brings responsibilities – and rewards. Both can be problematic, as the partnerships vividly demonstrate. Sean's complete possession of the months leading up to his death is an inspiring example of person-centredness within health and social care, and the ownership of all research processes and outcomes by the OPPS group is triumphantly evidenced within the legal contracts that accord all intellectual rights to older people and the commission that has invited them to future partnership. The 'official' reaction to The Long Distance Gang's success is interesting and demonstrates the sort of takeover bids that colonising organisations are infamous for. Equally off-putting are the detractions and prohibitions that suggest that Long Distance Gang members cannot possibly own the success of their film because of supposed lack of capacity. Here are clear examples of some of the put-downs to partnership described earlier in the Introduction.

In a growing space, people feel truly involved in the processes and outcomes of partnership and have a genuine sense of belonging and of ownership.

WHO TAKES THE CREDIT?

Sean Travers Lynch. October 30th 1944–February 4th 2011.
RIP.

There are some struggles to secure OPPS legal ownership of the research and its findings but finally the contract is bent in their favour. This will help ensure that older people and their supporters retain ownership of the research success and that powerful partners cannot salt away the credit or, significantly, the possibilities success opens up.

Reshma Patel reflects for PAct, on the other hand, how other people want a piece of her and her ideas:

> I have found that professional partners want to put me 'on show' as a 'project' – therefore making me feel that I have to do well. So my *own* feelings about whether I will be able to perform adequately become even more heightened. My personal thoughts about their motives are that all sorts of people enter into partnerships for all sorts of reasons – but they don't necessarily become a 'project!'

In my opinion, 'outside organisations' often try to monopolise my achievements and put me 'on show'. In actual fact, this happens in many partnerships that I am *supposedly* part of. I tick all the boxes for them in the ethnicity and disability categories. It is very important to be alert to the fact that organisations including funding bodies often try to take control and feed off our own hard work, as well as using us to demonstrate their commitment to diversity!

Good partnerships decide when, where and how to accredit themselves. Responsible partnerships share rewards and responsibilities. The best partnerships always give the credit where it honestly belongs.

Back to Oxford, in the 1990s! Advocacy In Action tell Chris Locke that they will not set up self-advocacy groups for him, but that they will ask people if they want to *set up their own partnerships*. It is very important to them that they do not colonise other people's experience in any way. Their partners get the full credit for the spaces they create. Advocacy In Action is just there to support them.

We also recall an ally in London who sees how the system works in terms of her partnerships with service users: '*they* jump through the hoops but *we workers* get the medals!'

We develop the notion of *colonisation* after others have stolen our own experiences. When a partner reads their ideas on 'peer advocacy' in *Enable Magazine* in 1990, he dashes off and writes a book on it. We don't mind at all as it proliferates a good principle. Nevertheless it is *our* principle. We feel sad that he has forgotten to mention how his big book is seeded from our little ideas, but we have come to know the parasitic partners that have fed on our experience and then proclaim themselves 'experts' on it. And we are consequently working on a repellent!

While acknowledging that there are trusting relationships enabling people to work together, June has also had disappointing experiences where some people within partnerships she has worked in have used service users to add to their own credibility:

For example, service-user organisations have appeared in the list of acknowledgements without their permission. It has happened that service-user organisations may have worked with others on a piece of work, but did not want to endorse the final report because they may not have agreed with its findings. However, they were never given the choice.

Not all pests in the garden are professionals, however. Service-user groups and activists can milk ideas too. Advocacy In Action members love the idea of spreading goodness, but for their own part, they try hard to credit everyone with their own ideas and actions. That's not to say they don't enjoy acknowledgement; they love it, but only if it is truly theirs for the taking!

React tried to ensure that all the children take credit for the success of the project. This supports the core aim to break down barriers of misunderstanding between disabled and non-disabled children:

> Everyone shares in the success of the project and everyone is equally rewarded by those who see the final performance. The pupils are given certificates to celebrate their achievements and these are shared in assemblies where the achievements of every child are acknowledged. The pupils all enjoy watching the video footage of their performances and show satisfaction through verbal acknowledgement, looking at themselves working, and smiling or reacting positively when they hear familiar sounds – for example, looking up when they hear a heavily percussive phrase which they had enjoyed each time they performed.

EMAPP also makes efforts collectively to ensure that all partners are given credit for the programme's success. As Jeanette comments: 'I think everyone takes the credit for the success of the partnership – hence the application for the Accolade'. It is the whole partnership that applies for a Skills for Care Accolade, whereas usual applications are from employers of social care workers. There is total agreement, among all members, that a joint application should be from service users, local authorities and the university.

Ed is trying hard to ensure that everyone takes the credit in his training company. For Ed this is partly to do with financial remuneration, but also about opportunities: 'At the moment Ed is paid… We want to pay everyone – but are working through benefit rules.' Success is also about everyone having a turn to learn new skills and share what they have achieved. Ed tries to make sure everyone gets a chance.

Stephen tries to conclude his partnerships by giving each person credit for their part in the assessment: 'The idea is that you walk away with them feeling that their opinions are welcomed and valued. It is important that their opinions are acknowledged and that they are thanked for their contribution.'

Celebrity follows exposure, and those partners who appear in The Long Distance Gang film get the applause *naturally*! But without a doubt, the credit is shared equally, as the extensive film credits themselves reflect. All accreditation is in alphabetical sequence rather than order of importance. (The reflections in this book equally belong not solely to those with the privilege of recording them but to the whole group.) Jon McGregor publicly commends Long Distance Gang joint collaboration in his *Guardian Weekend* article, Saturday 30th April 2011 (see p.177).

There *are* little disappointments, such as the cinema seafood fiasco, and an organisation that borrows *Arise, You Gallant Sweeneys!* for its own publicity and advancement, but overall The Long Distance Gang manages to celebrate, through joint presentations, tributes and rewards, the unequivocal value of everyone's involvement.

PAct members prefer accrediting participants in alphabetical order. This has sometimes been a major stumbling block for partnerships where there is strong pressure to name 'lead people' from the organisation or university. Community representatives see equal ownership as the most accurate and honest way of accrediting everyone where there has been equal effort.

Within APTCOO efforts are also made to ensure that people are given credit for what they have achieved: 'All take credit. It is important to the project that people's achievements are celebrated and acknowledged. This becomes a part of the culture of the project that everyone's successes are celebrated. This becomes the project's ethos'. Ensuring that credit is shared, and not just given to some, requires people within the partnership to be committed to make this happen. Trish talks about a culture being created within APTCOO. This is a crucial point. If efforts are not made so that everyone is included in celebration, then the result is what Julie, June and their colleagues have experienced at times – a marginalisation of some people at the advancement of others.

In summary

Reshma for PAct and June are both concerned when outside organisations and powerful partners steal credits they have not earned. Advocacy In Action and APTCOO are both very clear that credits should be shared for joint work.

Within a growing space people do not use one another, nor do they steal credit. People's work and the joint outcomes it produces are honoured and some do not take precedence over others in acknowledgement.

WHOSE WORKING STYLES?

People come into partnerships with familiar ways of behaving and working. In a healthy partnership, people are prepared to learn new ways of working with each other. The working styles that develop within partnerships should not be imposed by an individual or individuals but should be developed together.

Trish comments on how this has happened at APTCOO:

> The parents on the committee have adapted to working in a different way. A lot of new learning has taken place, so the new way of working is a natural development. The identity of the parents and the reason for being a part of the project is retained throughout this process so all feel comfortable with it. We aren't really aware of the changes in how we work at the time – it is how we evolve and develope as a group.

Advocacy In Action creates joint working styles in joint spaces.

> This means compromise for everyone – us included. Our preferred ways of working tend to be creative and enabling of self-expression. But not everyone feels comfortable with this. When Kevin invites a group of city leaders to take their ties off and sit on their paperwork, one man clutches his notes to his chest and stays buttoned up. Where Kevin says 'Be like me', this nervous partner apologises, 'I can only be like myself!' Here is so much learning for Advocacy In Action. We work hard to recognise what stops us or separates us in partnerships and then try to work around it to find shared solutions.

PAct members develop working styles that accommodate all within their various partnerships although this does perhaps inhibit the speed and method of reaching the final 'product'. There have been suggestions that this is compromised by quality, although experiences within PAct strongly suggest that quality is enhanced rather than reduced.

But notwithstanding, there are, lurking within the most comfortable of partnerships, the nettles that irritate and sting and remind us who is really 'in charge'. Julie recalls a university where service users develop and manage teaching and assessment. Some material is pictorial – hand drawn, the raw edge of people's experience. It shows that anyone can join in. But later, when the university itself is to be assessed by regulators, the visual aids are 'tidied up' with computerised images. Shocked and wounded, service users challenge the colonisation of their work. 'We must be seen to be *professional*,' the university responds.

PAct reflects how trickily the goal posts manipulate themselves. As Julie muses with regret, we can't take our eyes off them for a moment!

In Ed's training company great efforts are made to make sure that everyone is listened to and included in decisions. Members have to learn to work in new ways and Ed has to encourage new ways of behaving that people aren't used to, so the company had a professional image:

> Some people find some work boring and…do not do it…we are working together to try and get people to recognise their talents and develop those. Everyone has to learn that when representing the company they have to be professional – this at times is hard.

Although this way of working isn't as easily adopted as in Advocacy In Action or APTCOO, the same principle applies, that people develop new styles of working together.

Stephen sees many people for one-off assessments, and it is not possible for these short-term partnerships to develop more sustained ways of working together. But Stephen himself has developed a style of working as a result:

> When you are involved in short-term assessments, it might be the next service user who benefits from the learning. As an assessor you grow through every assessment. I know that I am getting better as an assessor but I also know that I can never be good enough. There is just so much to learn from each person I meet.

Throughout The Long Distance Gang's spaces, the emphasis stays on the person, not the 'condition'. And this shifts working styles firmly away from the 'medical model of cure, contain and control'. No one wants to be 'made better' in The Long Distance Gang, but may, however, choose to be the best they can when they feel like it.

Working styles bring together the practical with the conceptual, and blend head, hands and heart.

The strong group focus encourages and enables peer-driven values, plans and activity, where the looking after of one another and the responsibility to others override the interests of self. This does not create a dependence *on* the group but rather protects and empowers within it.

And those lovely bonds created by the group in Ireland 2008 tangle people together once more in the last rapid months of Sean's final journey, binding them even closer together in partnership.

Vulnerability is not part of the job description at '32', and 'workers' are not expected to have such intense ties with the 'residents' they support. But the crisis of Sean's illness and his death strip away the formal roles and expose a shared and naked humanity as people and partners first.

OPPS finds a gentle style that suits all, with lots of talking and reflecting and room for the shared experience of memories, hopes and dreams. Meetings proceed at a comfortable pace, with less formal spaces and dedicated 'work time'. OPPS tries to build up a culture of caring, sharing and mutual compassion and tolerance. However, as previously shown in relation to the group outcasts, members don't always get there!

In summary

Advocacy In Action expresses concern when their unique working style centred in the truth of their personal experience is 'tidied up' to satisfy the narrowed eyes of professional partners. Both OPPS and The Long Distance Gang celebrate peer-led and values-driven processes which, along with the Asperger's Consultation Group, focus on the whole person rather than the condition or the tick-box.

Within a growing space, partners are prepared to explore and adopt new ways of working which enable and celebrate everyone's contribution.

CAN DIFFICULTIES BE LEARNED FROM, OR DO THEY STAGNATE AND CAUSE BLIGHT?

Long Distance Gang mediation is very much in your face, or even 'on your face', as the sporadic black eye reveals! Problem-solving can be loud and angry, particularly when the beer is flowing. But everything out in the open is a good way to work — perhaps these bruises heal more healthily than the festering resentments that never get aired.

In looking back over the journey to death for Sean and those accompanying him, it is clear that engaging in a more open feeling way is liberating and healing. It frees up an erstwhile resistant worker to talk about loss in the worker's own life. It helps other partners understand her resistance in not wanting to get too emotionally involved and in endeavouring to remove palliative care away from her professional place of work.

And another worker comments on a conversation with a resident: 'I have worked with this man over any number of years – but never realised, until now, that he feels exactly the same way as I do, about death and dying'. In both these examples, bridges are built and crossed as people open themselves up to those around them. Getting in touch with our own fragility enables us all to reach out and touch others. But being this open is far from easy, and doubtless may be frowned upon by some. For the partnership, nevertheless, it stimulates immense collective growth, even through the processes of dying.

EMAPP has encountered various difficulties and differences of opinion over the years. It would be most surprising if it had not! But while such tensions have been stressful, work has been done to discuss the issues and to try and learn from them. Mick believes the partnership to be 'very effective in bringing lessons back to the table for discussion and future developmental work.' Jeanette agrees with this: 'I think that when difficulties occur they are used to learn from and I can point to several instances of this.'

PAct continues to reflect on all it has learned about joint activity, and members weigh up the challenges and opportunities around partnership working in the future.

Trish picks up on this theme when reflecting on how APTCOO has learned from difficulties:

> Over the years, the learning curve has been very steep for the committee so we have to learn from the 'downs' as well as the 'ups'. We can't afford to let things fester, so communication becomes key. As issues arise they are addressed either in the committee itself or outside of the meetings if this is more appropriate.

Reshma and Sherma agree that they cannot let difficulties fester: '…we don't allow anything to fester. We both feel that we can say if we feel uncomfortable with something. There are no hidden agendas because we have achieved a level of honesty.'

Ed recognises that it is not always easy to address difficulties: 'Problems are acknowledged – not always straight away – we try to offer support so people feel able to raise them appropriately.' OPPS is still working on its nasty little sore-spots of power, powerlessness and exclusion. They are opened up regularly and the partners try to heal the difficulties. But poison builds up again. It cannot be sorted over night. The trust and honesty between members allow them to revisit these painful places.

Advocacy In Action has encountered difficult partnerships over the years. Julie reflects that:

> Challenges around task-based activity are easier than those which are values-led, especially when partners find how each other ticks and how people like to co-work. But where activity is process or value-led, challenge is sometimes more personally, therefore *painfully*, received between participants and is more resistant to remedy.

Action based on values is particularly vulnerable to challenge, in that the confidence it inspires among partners is easily shattered when things appear to go wrong. Having taken the wrong turning out of the cloakroom and getting lost in the sprawling campus of the university, Anthony manages to elude Advocacy In Action for over an hour, until he is found, in the security office (where, having asked for help, he was taken), sitting happily drinking juice and wearing a peaked cap and an honorary university security badge! But rather than celebrate Anthony's survival skills, some student partners get angry. Their confidence in an entire morning's work exploring their values just crumbles, and they totally switch off from the whole notion of empowerment. One even says: 'we don't see why you need to feel in control, when you have us to look after you! We're here to make your lives better, not worse. It's what safeguarding is all about!'

Values-based challenge will put some partners at risk to such unfair repercussions. The problem is that the *values* themselves become vulnerable when mishaps occur. Here, there is a backlash of fury underlain by fear, and this then leads to a real risk of disintegration among emerging and fragile partnerships. It is not possible to say that such difficulties have been adequately dealt with for Advocacy In Action. But it is the *process* of exploring problems and solutions that now becomes crucial, and particularly the way that unrelated accidents and hitches are not allowed to poison the bigger truths, but can be learned from in a more positive manner.

In summary

The majority of the partnerships have faced difficulties head on, although OPPS has struggled with the discomfort of festering resentments and Advocacy In Action recognises it still has some work to do. PAct has experienced more disappointments within some of its more formal partnerships where much remains unsaid...

Within a growing space, difficulties are never ignored or allowed to compromise relationships. They are acknowledged and addressed, even welcomed at times, as they often lead to new perspectives, strengths, solutions and opportunities.

ARE PEOPLE FREE TO LEARN TOGETHER?

Perhaps it is the permissions within, as much as those outside, which affect our freedoms to learn. We need to *want* to learn, to realise that we *can* learn, and to admit that we learn well from others.

The Long Distance Gang band of travellers learn together, throughout their various journeys, across Ireland and later towards cinema celebrity. The confidence to learn and the realisation that others learn from them give some partners in particular a new strong understanding of their own abilities and value. But they are not always keen to admit it.

Sean remembers working from the age of six, cutting turf and tending the cattle. Schooling is a distant memory, soon over for the ten-year old boy sent to North America to labour for a family where: '...they fail to teach me a single thing except how to become a drunkard.' Sean drinks his childhood and teens away before coming to support his mother in England. The one thing life has taught Sean, he tells us, is that he cannot and will not change. And whenever life lands him a knock, he shrugs his shoulders, takes a slug from his can and repeats his elegy of surrender, 'Here I am on Broadway!'

But here is Sean, in the classroom, can in hand, telling his story to the students of social work. He wisecracks and weaves us from Ireland to America and on to the construction sites of Britain, as he tramps from one end of this country to the other in search of work in the 1960s and 1970s. With not one word of self-pity or regret!

> Sean strikes me as a charmer, funny and witty. I find it really hard not to cry. I save that till I get home.

...this changes how I view people — I need to look beyond the situation — 'dig deeper' — question why and how they get to this point — recognise and celebrate remarkable experiences.

I can't give up on the service users who may for whatever reason be harder to work with — Sean shows me that people are not only survivors but *achievers*.

So respond the students of the University of Nottingham, as they learn about life with Sean.

Sometimes, however, the knowledge generated in partnerships is not as great as it could be. Jeanette thinks that while learning together in EMAPP happens, practical concerns mean that it is not as good as it could be:

Well there are restrictions — what is possible within the University and local authorities at the time — resources, etc. — they restrict what can happen.

PAct conclude that:

What we learn from our experiences of formal alliances is that genuine relationships within good partnerships are not based on the professional nature of bureaucracy and paperwork, but simply on trust, hope, values and commitment.

OPPS findings expose the stark misery of loneliness, vivid patchworks of distant joy, pain, loss and achievement, and the modest simplicity of older people's future wishes — all of it intimately wrapped up within the vibrant power of personal statement. The research and group processes also demonstrate that older partners are not without skills and strengths simply because they are ageing; in fact, for some, *faculty*, in every aspect of the word, continues to be built on and developed. Finally, the partnership reveals that even where capacity is lacking, as in stages of dementia, older people are still able to co-work and to make genuine contributions. OPPS in all of these powerful ways is a real celebration of people learning with and from one another.

Advocacy In Action sees that service-user groups and other community activists do not necessarily share the same perspectives or aims and that it is indeed somewhat oppressive to lump everyone together and assume 'one single vision or one direction'. Often Advocacy In Action is asked to give the 'service-user perspective' when learning with and from other partners. Julie likes to talk about 'service-user communities' to emphasise this: '...there is no one "user perspective" – we are many communities, many people'. It is important to identify our differences and learn from them so that we can be united when we need to. Good partnerships enable this freedom of exchange.

On a practical level, it is communication, computer and life skills that Advocacy In Action workers trade with one another. Julie assists Stuart in discovering how to explore his feelings. Stuart employs his technology flair to help Julie learn the mysteries of the projector. Julie helps Brian improve his reading. Brian gives Stuart the knack of 'assessment'. Stuart helps Brian find out about medication. Brian works on Julie's understandings of Traveller culture. All of them say with one voice 'I'm not half so flummoxed these days, thanks to my colleagues' skill and patience.' The Asperger's Consultation Group also feel that they learn well together: 'We have a clear project direction and the group moves forward together.' They see the shared and agreed focus as providing a situation in which all members are able to learn together.

Ed highlights the issue of power in restricting the freedom to learn together:

> Sometimes people feel pushed in a direction by experts – Ed understands the reasons why legally we have to do certain things – other people sometimes find this difficult to understand and get frustrated. This has become more of an issue since the 'business' was formally set up – when it was informal this was less of an issue because everyone could choose more freely.

June observes that there are issues of power in other situations that restrict the learning that people can do together:

> It should be noted that this does not apply only to alliances which are made up of professionals and service users. Often there are tensions between service users and informal carers. Essentially these tensions increase when some allies do not understand and work to the Social Model in their alliance – these can be allies who are informal carers and/or professionals and even service users who still accept the Medical Model as the prime approach.

Julie, speaking for PAct, reflects on June's important comment, and adds:

> ...it is not only the prevalence of the Medical Model which can inhibit and suppress – equally power-depriving, although perhaps less apparent,

is the *redefining of our own ideas and values* by those who determine to hold on to the power. We must all be increasingly alert to this and prepared to challenge.

The emancipatory seeds of person-centredness and personalisation, germinated originally through the human rights protests of citizens with physical or learning disabilities and survivors of mental health services, appear on the face of it to have grown green and been grafted on as 'good practice' within mainstream provision of public and private health and social care agencies. But this is deceptive. Service provision has been unable on any large scale to yet truly replicate the original service-user vision and values. Paraded in its place, however, is a damaged and dangerous replica, disguised by the original language of promise.

And those of us within the movements who fought in the 1980s and 1990s for the inception of our values and ideals may presently find it difficult to acknowledge that things are not now working out as envisaged, for the most vulnerable and least powerful in particular. Indeed, some service users and service-user activists may actively cling to and promote the present illusion, blinkered to the 'reality behind the rhetoric', or bound by the belief that any change is better than no change at all. In this context, there is a danger that service users themselves may inhibit, and even work against, those very social and political models they have created or aspire to.

Where liberating concepts are so firmly trapped within rigid inward-looking frameworks that only the language remains to spell freedom, then it is indeed time for action. Otherwise decades of good energy and great ideas may just dissipate to dust.

'We live too fast and we die too quick.' This is one of Sean's immortal phrases from *Arise, You Gallant Sweeneys!*, and perhaps a fitting epitaph. After Sean's death, he lives on through his film. He wants his story told so that others can learn. At this time, it becomes vital to keep the partnership alive and in fact bring even more people in, as the urgency to support Gaynor to bury her father precipitates an urgent funding drive. Local Irish communities within the Mechanics and the Greyfriars pubs raised £1,500 from showing and selling the film. People learn together from responding to necessity. Sean himself, of course, would probably say he was beyond learning: 'Here I am on Broadway! That's me! I'll never change, I don't want to change.' Surely he's winding us up again!

In summary

Julie, for Advocacy In Action, and June, both reflect on the power issues that restrict learning and perception and how experience can be colonised and redefined within partnerships. Sean has shown that the blocks to learning can also sometimes come from within.

Within a growing space, partners have the freedom and the privilege to learn and to define new skills, new ways of understanding, and new ways of working together rather than some incorporating, subsuming or taking control of others.

Chapter **4**

BLOSSOMING AND PROLIFERATION

HOW DO PARTNERSHIPS MEASURE THEIR OWN SUCCESS?

If a partnership is successful, then this should be evident to those within it. People may not think about it in these terms, but they will feel valued and have a sense of achievement. The Asperger's Consultation Group (see p.20) see their success in two ways: 'We have produced good-quality work. We've formed friendships.' This shows that the group have been able to work well together and also that the process of working together has been such that the group members have not felt anxious and have been free to make friends.

Ed Morecroft and Sarah Craggs (see p.22) also emphasise the effectiveness of their partnership as well as the social aspects:

> We are still getting work – Ed is in demand, other people in the group have developed their skills and confidence and want to continue. People enjoy spending time together outside of work. Experts are keen to support the group even though times are tough and we have to downsize for a while.

Sarah and Ed also see continued interest in the group as a sign of its success as well as an opportunity to develop further: 'A new person has asked to join the group and this person will help us move into different areas – younger people.' For *React* (see p.30), success is measured in terms of how the children feel about working together and about each other:

At the end of the project, the pupils are able to communicate, socialise and work together extremely effectively. They have built friendships which were not there before and they are able to express themselves in new ways. The first project aim was to build opportunities for interactive, creative and independent expression. All the pupils are able to work together creatively and carve their own performance, which reflects their personalities and newly formed friendships. The pupils with disabilities are able to influence the world around them through use of digital technology and creative collaboration with their partners. The final performance piece is a tribute to this, and the way that everyone worked together was truly inspiring. Another aim of the project was to promote positive relationships with and understanding of pupils' strengths and individuality from both schools. When interviewed at the end of the project, the pupils from Colebourne are enthusiastic about their peers from Beaufort School. One pupil reflects: 'I really like Sam. She's like the happiest child in the world and she makes everyone smile because she's always smiling.'

Pupils are also able to acknowledge strengths in their peers with or without disabilities, making comparisons between James, who does not have a disability, and Haidar, who is unable to walk independently, because they both move 'really fast'.

Long Distance Gang (see p.24) outcomes are not measurable or time linked, but for individual partners are about confidence, self-esteem and personal growth, a slow fruition through which people come to know themselves in firmly rooted ways, as people of worth and capacity who have an impact on the spaces they occupy and the others in them. Joe and Tom move to live at '32'. Pat goes on the tram to town each day. Sean and Tom spend Christmas with Julie. Kitty and Patricia become regular visitors at '32' and spoil everyone rotten with cabbage and bacon and Irish stew. Julie and Nes plot some new ideas. Sean assesses students on a Master's degree programme. Everyone grows fuller, richer lives.

The group itself experiences an organic 'morphing' over three years, from motley gatherings around songs and memories to a united band of determined travellers and yet again into film-makers, philosophers and presenters.

The public success of *Arise, You Gallant Sweeneys!* is an unplanned-for and unexpected bonus. The film, as a space for people to tell their stories, makes important journeys and heals past wounds, and has served its purpose for the partners. No one could have dreamed it would have such an impact on others. But the audiences laugh until they cry and then weep in earnest. Jon McGregor, in his notes for the *Guardian Weekend* article (Saturday 30th April 2011), describes:

> ...a film to move you to tears if you let it, and to make you shake your head at the pity of two failed economies – the one with no work for its young people, the other so heavily reliant on cheap exploited labour without any thought of what men might do when they reach the end of the road, but it's not a film that sets out to do either of these things: rather it's a film that sets out to tell the story of an ambitious and difficult journey – in the way that the men who feature in it would have it told. No more and no less.

The film and its presenters also have a deep impact on policy-makers, students and practitioners, inviting them into the partnership, where they are motivated to build their own growing spaces with the people they support.

Reshma Patel and Sherma Patel (see p.31) measure their success by how they are able to work together in different situations:

> When we take this partnership to different situations, such as working together on teaching, we are able to work in a way that involves us both at every stage.

Sherma encourages Reshma to make links with her own experience and the teaching. This results in very positive feedback from students, who see the benefit of true partnership working.

> We work on everything together. When we co-work we are sensitive to each other's needs and we are able to adjust to respond to each other's needs, which makes the working relationship 'flow'.

In measuring achievements over the final six months of Sean's life, Nes considers:

> ...the enhanced levels of understanding among the staff and the lengths to which workers are prepared to go to support us, and which now spill over and beyond existing care home job requirements and what might reasonably be expected from any organisational staff team.

Dave celebrates:

> ...the day Sean dies...open grief and sadness...permission granted... Julie, Gaynor, grandchildren...Nes...residents and staff — extremely powerful and significant.

Julie reflects on:

> ...a great shared birthday, good talks with students, the trip back home, some loving kinship ties, a wonderful Christmas day, one final pub crawl in the last week of life, death surrounded by family and true friends, the local cathedral filled with mourners from Ireland and England, and with all the men from '32' so dignified in their suits, the Irish flag on the coffin and an Irish graveside lament, and finally, through the subsequent 'adoption' of Gaynor and her three children — the ongoing spirit to support others.

Mick Regan adds:

> My great mate Sean. I'm gonna miss him.

What would Sean himself want to say here? What success is there for Sean in death? We can only respectfully guess. His early words hold the key:

> ...this is who I am — don't try and change me just because I'm dying!

The directive is fully honoured, Sean!

Again, the relationship built up as a result of working together in partnership is crucial to its ultimate success. For Stephen Vickers (see p.32) also, even though he only meets each individual probably once, this is still really important:

> Even if the decision is not the outcome someone would have necessarily wanted, you *know* whether they have engaged with you. If you walk away having learned from them and they have been able to share their perspective, you can count it as something of a success. You may not be the person who revisits, so you don't always know the outcome and it is therefore about the here and now and getting that link and them feeling that they can share that with you in some way.

Others see the success measured in terms of recognition. Mick cites the recognition received by the East Midlands Adults PQ Partnership (EMAPP) (see p.21) as a sign of the partnership's success:

...recently acknowledged as Skills for Care Accolade Finalist 2010 regarding effective partnership working and continued professional development of social care workers.

For Jeanette, from the same partnership, success is measured by the fact:

...that it is still there and continues to be valued by everyone. That we have evolved and taken on new strands.

The fact that this partnership isn't just standing still but is prepared to take on new challenges means that people are not complacent but really want to continue to provide a good learning experience for the candidates on the programme.

Trish Green measures the success of A Place to Call our Own (APTCOO) (see p.18) in terms of practical achievements, the achievement of fulfilling their 'wish list' and not changing their value base:

We have our own building to meet in and this has validated our identity and made the project seem more real. We have supported hundreds and hundreds of families throughout Nottinghamshire. We now deliver services and support groups that parents have identified a need for. We work in a multiagency way supporting carers in accessing and challenging services. We have fulfilled our wish list – the aims and objectives we identified as parents.

We have been true to our core values. We feel that our voice is heard by other agencies. This might not always be comfortable for other agencies, especially when we are challenging them, but we are respected. We have built up a sense of community for the parents who then develop a sense of belonging. We are aware that this could feel exclusive to some, so we have worked hard at being open to new people.

The confidence and pride of the Older People's Partnership Services (OPPS) researchers (see p.27) and their peer-elders who agreed to be interviewed says it all: 'We have built this up – this is all our work!' The publication of a glossy professional report and an executive summary in various translations officially recognises the group's achievement. Success of the research is evidenced by the Leicester City Council's full adoption of its recommendations and, in a time of cuts and crisis, by the securing of ongoing funding for OPPS to co-produce and implement an action plan for services to older people in Leicester.

Mary sees the growth of strength and confidence apparent in OPPS, and celebrates the trust engendered in older service users by their researcher peers. She praises the development of OPPS as a cohesive group with a valuable contribution, and credits the ability of the group to relearn or learn skills even where thought by some to be impossible. She highlights the mutual empowerment of both researchers and the researched, and particularly values the ability of this research to get to the heart of people and to capture real lives. Mary finally acclaims a task completed and results achieved, and the development of OPPS as a partnership with purpose.

In respect of the inner workings of OPPS, however, group ties are not as strong as they could be. Is this an indicator of the outer dynamics, that the group has been put together for the purposes of others? After a period of absence, it is difficult to revive the same interest when reconvening the group for stage two. In the unfunded months, people lose focus, although they keep in touch and meet informally. If OPPS is truly an alliance between providers and users, then success will depend in the long term on more firmly rooted links between partnerships that are not vulnerable to being ripped up by lack of funding.

Advocacy In Action, meanwhile, has stood the course of time well, and reflects back on some success:

...other partners come to learn with us. We team up with community workers and play workers, priests, politicians and architects – anyone! We work with schools and churches and meet with rights groups and unions. We go to Italy and Slovenia, while India comes to us through the British Council when disabled workers fly to England to learn at our side. Our works, pictures, videos, are known from Canada to India to Australia. We win national and international awards.

And in over two decades, we have met thousands of partners in hundreds of alliances. We have assisted and enabled over one hundred other service-user and community groups. We do not set up new 'Advocacy In Actions' – we help people decide what sort of a partnership they want for themselves – and we still remain in touch as their allies.

Much work is with universities and local authorities and is about promoting *genuine* partnership and involvement and helping people in shared learning settings to feel confident to work together as practitioners and users of services.

Increasingly we are developing partnerships based on our early understanding that professional allies and service users are *mutual survivors* of social control regimes. We have now learned to jointly resist, challenge and redefine unyielding service frameworks. We have also learned to value one another as 'equally experienced'.

Advocacy In Action members come and go as they wish. Some people still remain from the 1990s. Newcomers bring new ideas and opportunities. Advocacy In Action likes to see itself not so much as a fixed group but more as a way of working together within a number of possibilities. There is now an open flowing network of partners in and out of activity, and support is dictated by the needs and aspirations of the partnership and its individuals.

Personal success for co-workers is reflected by housing of choice, marriage and partnerships, jobs, official appointments and appearances, publications and television programmes, and by a lovely sense of *who we are* as whole human creatures. A colleague remarks that 'people have grown taller' – her inner vision has taken in the fullness of our being.

We try to bring this into the spaces we create with allies, to model a freer, healthier way of being together within partnerships. The riotous and blossoming profusion of wonderful new ideas and action are the ultimate measure of success for participants. What better soil for generating growth, than digging deep into our own experience!

In summary

A huge measure of success within all the alliances is the growth within people. These processes of emancipation and personal development are less easy to quantify than the commodified outputs of more target-driven partnerships and may not hold the same kudos. Notwithstanding, Advocacy In Action, Ed's business, *React*, APTCOO, OPPS, EMAPP and The Long Distance Gang have all produced significant and innovative contributions within the arenas of health and social care and the arts that place them at the forefront of new ideas and solutions.

In a growing space, success is measured not solely on hard targets, but also celebrates personal outcomes and processes of engagement and growth.

HOW HAVE PEOPLE BEEN ABLE TO REFLECT TOGETHER ABOUT WHAT THEY HAVE LEARNED?

Advocacy In Action brings reflection into all its spaces. 'It is one of our guiding principles and we make time for it. We help their partners to consider with us.' This book contains many such reflections. Advocacy In Action are proud of their work with the University of Nottingham, to graft reflective practice into the programme from recruitment and selection to teaching, assessment and placement learning in social work. They reflect on all that they do as part of its process.

It is not always possible to have meetings that allow for such reflection to take place owing to time constraints, so if this is an issue then it is a good idea to provide opportunities outside of main meetings for this to take place. Mick from EMAPP sees these additional times as valuable for reflection:

> Academic partners organise developmental days to provide both opportunities to reflect and ensure standardisation across the programme.

The dual purpose of time for reflection that Mick alludes to is also highlighted by Trish in talking about APTCOO:

> We have to monitor and evaluate what we do because we don't want to lose the sense of achievement and the successes that we have. It is important for the new Board of Directors to be aware of all the good work that takes place.

PAct (Our Promise to Act) (see p.29) members experience sadness when partnerships do not invest some time to find and pluck out the thorns, which then go on to fester. Lack of reflection contributes to an 'unfinished' feeling which relates less to what has been said than to that which remains unsaid. Formal partnerships often talk about lack of time but are less keen to talk about its *impact*. PAct members reflect on and learn from this.

Minutes to OPPS meetings are fully reflective of process as well as activity. Each meeting itself ends with five minutes for feedback and appreciations. The OPPS research report devotes serious space to reflecting on the partnership as well as the findings. All partners reflect on the visits and the interviews, and on the situations of older people and their responses, and learn much from their experience:

…too little social support and too much protection — who is it all for?

…older people often have queries or concerns they are reluctant to bring up for fear of repercussions, or of being seen as a nuisance. One of the most important things the research group has done is to make service users feel comfortable enough to talk openly with us.

…the greatest positive of the research for me has lain in the joy of our older people having someone to talk to, as they discuss with us their lives and their home care. To experience the joy of the sharing of their life stories with us, their appreciation that they are not forgotten and to know our visit has in some small way helped to break the isolation and loneliness.

Politicians and providers also reflect with OPPS and learn much at the launch event, particularly while the older people spoon-feed these powerful partners with yoghurt:

…being fed, powerless, humiliated, no control — loss of control, vulnerable, dependent. What if yoghurt spills on my dress? I have to meet people later! What if they get it on my face? I have this compulsion to want to 'take over' — so I keep my hands behind my back.

Delegates tell OPPS members that they find the impact of what has been shared to be very powerful and thought-provoking and have learned from it: '…no presenter mentions "being protected" as a good aspect of care! How true! Local authorities and independent providers, take note!'

The best Long Distance Gang reflections take form through clouds of thick tobacco smoke and over a pint or two. In the years before his death, Sean, the philosopher of the group, along with side-kick Mick Regan, often chewed over events and outcomes of the 2008 journey in the 'wet lounge' at '32' where Julie and Nes are frequent visitors.

In lovely safe spaces of our own choosing, we reflect on the power of friendships and the need for them to continue under all sorts of circumstances, on the importance of trust and loyalty, on how history repeats itself and on the need to learn from it, on the disgrace of being discarded, on the joy of belonging, and on the power of telling our own story.

When asked if they are able to reflect together, the Asperger's Consultation Group states 'Yes, and we take great pride in what we are doing.' For this partnership, the opportunity to talk together about the experience of having Asperger's, and the issues that people encounter, is a really important part of the group experience. 'The importance of listening to shared experience' is evident. Not all the group members know anyone else with Asperger's before joining the group and so they are able to 'learn about having Asperger's at different times in life', and see that people can live successfully and happily. They are able to support each other in meetings through just talking openly about how they feel: 'We have been positive role models for each other.'

In reflecting together on what people have learned from the months before death, night staff recall talking with Sean through his final weeks, often in the small hours of the morning, when together they ponder on what living and dying mean to them.

The men of '32' down their cans in the 'wet room'. They revisit the sessions at Sean's bedside, prior to his death. Mick Regan, soul mate and confidante, relates how they looked back over many shared benches, many shared cans and many shared experiences. It is to Mick that Sean whispers the words he wants on his gravestone: 'Gach rud ar son an ghrá – all for love.'

Julie, Dave and Nes spend long hours in reflective spaces and reach the following understandings:

> ...we firstly recognise and own our personal vulnerability – and we accept that resilience lives hand in hand with it.
>
> We know there are issues in the safeguarding of older people, those assessed as 'lacking in capacity' – those in society seen as vulnerable. However, there can be no excuse ever for disregarding the right to live a whole and wished for life up to the moment we die.
>
> We seek signs of safety, and opportunity, within a climate of belief in and hope for one another. We are not blinkered, but alert to the risk signals. We know we can buffer with the wise protection that absorbs shocks, without preventing those necessary bumps and collisions people meet and survive in life. And we uphold the right to make wise or unwise decisions and learn from them.
>
> Where controls must be strict, and outcomes fixed, then the journeys crucially must be dignified.
>
> We accept that journeys can be unplanned for and unwanted – but we want to make sense of our journeys and help one another do the same – to understand *how* we reach points in our lives, how to move forward from them, and how to know when the end is in sight.

In summary

Much time is given to reflection within these pages and within the partnerships they describe. Groups such as Advocacy In Action, OPPS and Ed's trainers allocate quality time to reflecting on and learning from experience. Dave, together with Julie, Nes and all at '32', look back on the Ireland trip and more recently on Sean's final months and recognise how much wisdom they have accrued along the way. Partnerships that are too busy to reflect neglect this process at their own cost.

In a growing space, people make the time and the freedom to reflect on both their achievements and what working together has taught them.

PROPAGATION AND DISPERSAL

If a partnership is valuable to those in it, then this may well inspire others and thus good models of partnership working can help to influence other partnerships. The Asperger's Consultation Group would like this to happen:

> We are not at that point – but hope to be inspirational to others.

Part of the motivation for being part of this group is to show other adults with Asperger's and everyone else what they can achieve together.

OPPS want to tell lots of people about their group and their research and especially about the lives of older people who need care and support. *Listen to Me – I Live Here*, the OPPS research report, has been made widely available through its website, at www.leicester.gov.uk/your-council-services/social-care-health/older-people/listen-to-me-i-live-here-report.

Team assistant, Amita, is particularly deeply affected by her OPPS partners: '…you've helped me to better understand the issues confronting older people and I'm determined not to let that go to waste. The OPPS group has been such a wonderful teacher.'

Julie, for PAct, reflects that service-user involvement is highly complex and rides on a set of liberating values that may not sit comfortably within restricted processes and settings. At its best, involvement empowers workers and users within problem-solving partnerships that celebrate the contribution of each towards wished-for and lasting solutions. At its worst, 'involvement' is just something than professionals 'do' to their clients.

Jeanette, from EMAPP, wants to use the lessons about partnership working in other situations: 'I hope people have taken the lessons from the partnership and used them in their organisations – I have and I think others have too.'

The partners of Sean Travers Lynch live on, but are changed in the knowledge of him. The seeds of the partnership have quickened in everyone's hearts and minds and have flourished through the regard they hold to one another and within the new spaces they will go on to create. It is too soon since Sean's death to measure how far the good will travel.

Ed's work is inspirational to others: 'Other authorities ask Ed how he does it. Other people with a learning disability say they want to be like Ed – younger people with a learning disability.'

There is only one Advocacy In Action and this is how it should be. But other partners can take from it what works for them and adapt it to their own purposes.

Many of our ideas are used quite widely, and this makes us feel deeply proud, but humbled also. We feel a great responsibility to be the best we can, while other people look to us as role models.

There was a time when their involvement was not so welcome. Advocacy In Action recalls the fury of a day services manager in the 1990s who threatens to sue his service users when they complain about their day centre. The self-advocacy programme funding is stopped across the county as a result. But now there are groups all over the world where Advocacy In Action can claim some part in their development.

The work of Jeeja Ghosh in Calcutta adapts Advocacy In Action ideas and processes to develop performance theatre for Indian people with disabilities and university partners. New groups in the mountains of Northern Italy give their own teaching to students and practitioners after Advocacy In Action involve them as presenters with the partners.

The work of Kevin Chettle is widely celebrated; his pictures never fail to move. Nowadays, they also provide a familiar and multi-coloured front on the cover of many an academic publication. Kevin's art gives these works the stamp of approval, because, of course, it only adorns the books that celebrate good partnership!

Advocacy In Action are keen to know how their ideas are taken up and used by others. Mark Lymbery reflects on the impact on students and staff, believing it has 'fostered significant points of growth and learning', and he summarises that in respect of students:

> …any person wishing to be an effective social worker must have a good appreciation of the lives of others – their experiences, the pressures and strains that have been placed on them, their humanity and resilience. The exposure to the lives of service users in teaching sessions creates a good opportunity for students to hone their empathic skills and should help to ensure that they retain a critical sense of service users as fully rounded human beings when they become practitioners. In addition, the student experience of presenting an aspect of their (own) lives puts them in touch with the emotions of service users who are expected to be able to reveal – often repeatedly – the most painful of memories and experiences to social workers.

Mark considers how Advocacy In Action's messages have an impact on academic staff:

> …however skilled, there are few university-based social work lecturers who have the ability and knowledge to enable students to share accurately in the life experiences of service users. In addition, breaking down the barriers between students and service users also has an effect for university staff. In general terms, it enables staff to model personal behaviours and attributes that are particularly appropriate for social work education.

Advocacy In Action wonders whether its ideas and messages will stand the test of time. They always like to ask people what they took away from their involvement when they meet them, years later.

> One day we bump into someone we remember as an enthusiastic young student from the University of Birmingham. 'Can you recall any of the learning?' he is asked. '…the messages never leave me,' Jon Glasby tells us. 'They inform my practice in every way.' People ask us back again and again. Students become managers and then use the ideas to spread good practice. In this way our work seems to just grow and grow.

One problem for Advocacy In Action has been the absolute lack of time to sit down and put thoughts to paper. Over the years they have been seen as the action people – *advocacy* and *action*! Now perhaps is the right time to propagate and disperse their ideas, through books like this one.

APTCOO, through time, inspires many people:

Over the years, other groups and agencies want to come and see what we are doing and learn from our good practice. They also want to learn about the *pitfalls* and the challenges that we have. We are happy to share this knowledge with others. With other parents, we hope that they don't feel on their own, although we are aware that there are parents who don't access our service – we are there if they need us though.

Stephen is similarly aware of the importance of modelling good practice as well as teaching it:

If I can communicate the lessons that I have learned to others, they will take that and apply these lessons to their own practice. They too can share with me. Leading by example is important. Being passionate, enthusiastic and going the extra mile will inspire others. Leading from the front and showing people that you care is really important.

Staff partners take the spirit of The Long Distance Gang film and the Ireland journey to their hearts, where it stays. Workers consider its deep impact on the way they see their relationships with the older men:

It's more than just a day's work; these are people's lives. It motivates us to reclaim our determination to help people achieve what they *want* to achieve and to begin to celebrate potential rather than focusing on inability or need.

The Long Distance Gang's film travels widely to spread knowledge to learners and practitioners and the general public. It also helps people link into their personal emotions, memories and experiences:

I'm ashamed to say I first feel sorry for them, pity, I don't notice, I merely judge by what I see. But as the film goes on, I see the inner strength of the characters, it makes me realise just how judgemental I really am and that's hard to come to terms with. Now I hear the pride in their voices. I understand how they need to keep their independence.

Release of the film renders it open to opinion, which can dilute or distort the values and intent and skew the experiences. This makes the partnership at risk to compromise, only in that it becomes other people's property in how they choose to receive and replicate its ideas. However, The Long Distance Gang feel confident in carrying the ideas themselves and assisting others to propagate them. They proudly give out their contact details for the DVD: outsidefilm@mail.com, for information on *Arise, You Gallant Sweeneys!*

Reshma and Sherma see the benefit of lessons they learn together being shared with the social work student whom Reshma goes in to support and assess:

The student hasn't recognised different identities and doesn't see Reshma as a service user but Reshma is able to support her to see this identity as a direct result of the learning that has happened in her partnership with Sherma. It inspires the student's practice as she then sees service users as experts in their own right. It really challenges the concepts of power.

In summary

True involvement and partnership produces lots of 'lovely off-shoots', as many of the partnerships describe, because they have momentum and energy.

The growing space is that which enables the principles of good partnership to transfer to new places and possibilities and to take root there.

BEING CREATIVE

When partnerships work well they are creative. Mark Lymbery believes that investing the working time to enable trust and confidence within his alliance with Advocacy In Action has enabled true creativity to blossom and make the University of Nottingham a trail-blazer throughout the last 20 years, in involving communities in the education of the practitioners and policy-makers who aim to serve them:

We have been able jointly to build creative approaches to the involvement of service users in social work education. From the starting point of self-contained teaching sessions, we have been able to move into various aspects of assessment – of student presentations, of students' readiness to undertake practice learning, of candidates' appropriateness to be offered places on the social work course, etc.

Working without funding hones the keen edge to seize 'commercial opportunity' to build up new and creative spaces, as individuals, as a group and within all wider partnerships. And remaining unpaid as workers ensures that whatever Advocacy In Action does is for the sheer joy or necessity of it. The money earned enables them to provide free services to people, groups and communities with restricted income. This empowers them in their turn to be creative with confidence!

Experiences within PAct confirm that creative use can be made of the most limited resources and still produce something important. Gina, Julie and Kevin reflect on materials and programmes they have produced without a budget, using nothing other than their own experiences that have engaged the interest and secured the commitment of generations of students and practitioners across the country.

For Ed and Sarah, their creativity, in the way they work, has wider influences: 'We make other organisations think about way they do their work, e.g. tenants surveys.' Creativity truly is the key to good learning and good partnerships.

This different way of 'doing things' means that partnerships can move away from traditional approaches and re-focus what they do to be consistent with their values. Trish comments:

> We provide a different focus to other services. Our support is about the whole family and this could include the extended family. We don't turn any family away that has a disabled child, so there is no complex referral form or strict eligibility criteria.
>
> Parents as experts is at the core of everything that we do.

APTCOO is not confined by the same organisational constraints as other agencies, and so is able to work in a way that they know as parents is better for the families they support.

The Asperger's Consultation Group is creative in the way that its members work together and benefit from each other's company, opinions, experiences and friendship. Part of the *stereotype* of people with Asperger's might suggest that they may not be able to work in this way, but they want to challenge this perception. A group member comments that 'People with Asperger's *can* form working partnerships. The Asperger's Consultation Group is a positive example of showing the good sides of Asperger's. It makes me more inclined to do further work like this.' The group see future possibilities: 'there are lots of different areas about Asperger's that could do with some researching'.

The partnership between Reshma and Sherma is another partnership set up to challenge accepted ways of operating. What develops as something new is:

...the idea of service users being mentors for other service users to support students in their learning. Reshma plans to take on this role and the idea is for Sherma and Reshma to jointly deliver the Enabling Learning module for service users.

But they comment sadly: 'However, the funders have withdrawn their support and changed the emphasis on service-user involvement in educating social work students.'

Sean, Nes, Julie, Dave, the workers at '32' and a growing number of volunteers start to find real solutions outside of, albeit often in partnership with, traditional services. As funding cuts begin to eat into formal provision, the need to work creatively with voluntary and community partners burgeons into urgency.

June also says that the wider agenda is affecting alliances that have been strong:

> The increasingly risk-aversive position of statutory bodies affects service-user involvement to the point that we are going back to it being a tick-box exercise. In social work education, alliances have developed over many years with Higher Education Institutions and local authorities. However, where previously service users who are trained and experienced practice educators have been accepted to undertake this role, they will soon not be able to continue.

June holds the Practice Teaching Award and has taught and assessed students in their practice learning settings for 16 years. She considers it a great loss to the development of students' learning to exclude this experience and expertise, particularly as it is 'rooted in the service-user understandings'.

So, even when partnerships operate very creatively and push existing barriers, sometimes wider agendas can stop this creativity.

Stephen works in situations that have the potential to stifle creative practice, so he tries to find imaginative ways of working with people:

> You get creative yourself in searching for what is in the person's best interest. I ask myself what can we do within legal frameworks to get the best for a person? What are they entitled to? And how can I advocate that they get it? What I have learned then goes into training others so they too can go that extra mile.

Seeing that assessing people brings a 'richness' is the first step to being creative – it is a motivator for finding ways of making a link with someone and including them as far as is possible in any decisions made about them.

Nes reflects with Julie on the three-year process, on how planning and executing a brave journey and producing a film, have opened up The Long Distance Gang to the most creative of shared decision-making: '...the voyage is and remains a space over which the group has full control and the resultant film is not owned by any individual but collectively by all of its participants.' The partnership depends very little on paperwork but greatly on the sharing of stories. The stories are turned into film and teaching materials. And in 2011, the group creatively use the film to fundraise for Sean's burial, bringing local communities and their goodwill into the partnership.

In summary

June, Reshma and Sherma are wary of the restrictions that can be placed on true creativity within partnerships more driven from the outside. Advocacy In Action and other community-led alliances celebrate the creativity and inventiveness that passionate commitment inspires, notwithstanding limited resources.

A growing space encourages and seeks out innovation and inspires the allies within it to push the creative boundaries further and further.

GOOD MODELS OF PRACTICE IN PARTNERSHIP WORKING

...partnership is very simple and works well for us. It depends on us truly seeing one another – how we are – and how we could be.

So says everyone in The Long Distance Gang!

It is important to the Asperger's Consultation Group that they organise the way they work and are able to work at their own pace. Their work is organised in a very logical way, with one stage building on the stage before. They also decide themselves how they want meetings recorded. Initially discussions are written on to flipchart paper, and these are typed up. Later on, group members type directly on a laptop so they can all agree what is recorded at the time. For this partnership the way they work together 'grows organically; we are not restrained within a framework. We do what comes naturally.'

For those left behind, in the wake of Sean's passing, work carries on: 'alcohol and health workers are keen to work with Dave and take this partnership as a model.' The Sean Travers Fund is set up to ensure burial with dignity.

OPPS gives us many lessons, in linking into thoughts and feelings, in how to see beyond the surface in order to value one another, and in how to work with passion, possibility and hope. Practitioners reflect on their engagement with older people:

> What I will take forward into practice is to look at myself, to remember to be honest and respect each individual. I don't want to erase what I feel as a human being. I want to gain understanding, and learn what people's thoughts and feelings really are, and I want to make honest time to listen.

> These people were my age once. It scares me about how I might end up. But again probably I am at fault in only seeing what I want to see. I recognise that older people have much to offer, amazing experiences and knowledge to inform others. They have a rich tapestry which is an untapped resource to be respected and admired.

The way EMAPP members work in partnership in designing the programme sets the tone for all other aspects. Mick highlights what is important to him about the partnership working practice:

> Shared learning, respecting and valuing all parties as experts in their own areas of knowledge and understanding. Mirroring our partnership approach across the design and delivery of the programme, ensuring learning is consistently reflected in the design and development of programme content.

For Jeanette, in talking about the same partnership, 'The model of good practice is to value everyone and use people's strengths to help them to grow and participate.'

Members of PAct believe they have learned through doing, viewed mistakes as an opportunity for reflection and improvement and now intend to move principles into practice.

PAct associate Reshma Patel advocates for long-term allegiances:

Partnerships of the best variety are, for me, created over a long time. The partnership bus should not be one where people are picked up and then dropped off again. Partnerships are about *wanting* to work together and being given room to grow naturally, rather than being 'forced' to fruition.

Stephen describes his model of good practice in assessing people who don't have capacity about what is in their best interest: '...building on a shared understanding.' He explains:

Working in this very constrained way and within tight deadlines in an intense set of circumstances make the importance of working in partnership magnified. You are aware of the substance of the decision because you know the seriousness of the outcome. You have to be aware of this all of the time. The day you forget this will be the day you don't act in the best way for people. It is an enhanced experience of partnership working.

Mark Lymbery reflects on the aspects of Advocacy In Action's work he shares, through collaborative partnerships with them to develop teaching and learning in social work:

I am diffident about advancing benefits for service users; they can and will speak for themselves. However, I have witnessed the regrowth of their confidence when sharing difficult aspects of their lives. It seems to have allowed them to reclaim a sense of power and control that they had lost – often through a sequence of very poor practice. I have also been struck by the ability of people to make a strong emotional connection with the student group.

The partnerships between social work learners and those affected by social work services and social control systems have radicalised social work education. Mark applauds such alliances:

This is the critical issue for me – the involvement of service users in the education of successive generations of social work students has improved their capacity to function as effective practitioners (as well as being the morally correct thing to do). It provides a 'growing space' that enables this to happen. Of course the process imports challenges and pressures, but the benefits to all parties fully justify the struggle.

A student reflects on the model of learning and partnership she takes from Advocacy In Action:

I realise the degree to which I have cut myself off and become numb and have taken my knowledge for granted. I can now, and will now, link into my own experience to understand and enable others. I will pass on my experience and knowledge to others just as Advocacy In Action has done for me. Knowledge and experience are there to be shared by all. Advocacy In Action has helped me know what services *feel* like.

It is hard for me to admit that my practice, though good at times, has not been great at others, in fact crap at times. I don't think anyone likes to be wrong, but I've learned more from my assumptions and my own prejudices than from any book.

Trish sees the good model of partnership working for APTCOO as being concerned with not losing the focus on families and also being able to operate at a professional level so that families can benefit from other partnerships. She reflects how:

> ...we develop a professional and corporate image but at the same time retain our values and are able still to offer the emotional support to families of disabled children. We develop the ability to present in two ways – one is our 'softer' face which we present to families – and the second is the 'professional' 'suit and make-up' face which we need to present to the professional world to be taken seriously and to achieve what we want to achieve.

Similar to Reshma and Sherma, Trish has an example of excellent practice in partnership working which becomes a victim to policy agenda and funding changes:

> For a few years a team is set up which includes social care, health and education workers and this team is co-located with APTCOO. This is set up for disabled children and, while it runs, it works very well. Professionals are faced with parents who access APTCOO whom they are working with in accessing services in their workplace. Most of the professionals rise to the challenge and this improves working relationships between parents and professionals and breaks down some of the perceived barriers between them. Sadly, owing to funding issues, this does not continue and the workers return to their previous office bases. This is a real shame as we lose a model which serves families much better.

In summary

The models of partnership and engagement within this book have not allowed themselves to be incorporated, colonised or commodified.

Within a true growing space, people can eloquently express why and how their partnership works for them and will champion it against the detractors who try to dismiss or devalue what they do not understand. However, complacency has no place here, and the growing space is always on the look out in case poor practice tries to seed itself.

LEARNING ABOUT YOURSELF IN PARTNERSHIP WORKING

It's my personal journey too. It's all about where life is taking me as I edge towards 60. It's a hanging onto control as I too become older, vulnerable and time-limited. This research is a validation of who I am as an older person, what I believe in, where I intend to go with my ageing – and how I intend to travel! (Julie Gosling, research consultant)

OPPS support worker, Reshma, learns about some constraints on her willingness to share opinion in collaborations with more powerful OPPS partners: 'As a person who uses services indirectly provided by the local authority, I don't feel I'd be able to hold my stance during any tensions, for fear of losing services.'

Researcher Joyce sees her own life and others more clearly:

I feel that my eyes have been opened and I believe I am wiser for being a part of OPPS. I'm a better person because of what I've done and seen. My confidence has grown tremendously. Never in my wildest dreams did I imagine I could have been a part of something like this. If you'd have told me 18 months ago what I'd be doing now, I'd have laughed.

Researcher for OPPS Chandrika Singh appreciates how 'It gives me confidence. It keeps me occupied. Basically it's developed me. And it keeps the grey cells growing. Such a relief from all the caring!'

People recognise they can achieve individually and together through partnership, and that life is about growing, no matter what age you are.

When we work closely with others in partnerships we learn much about them but we also learn about ourselves. Asperger's Consultation

Group partners learn that what they think is important, and also that *they* are important: 'We've learned that we have something important to say. I've learned that I deserve to be heard.' They realise this through 'trusting each other and depending on each other. Our differences when we work together make us stronger.'

When Sarah and Ed think about their partnership, they see they have learned quite similar things. They have both learned self-belief. Sarah knows 'to trust myself even if organisational pressures make this difficult.' Ed knows 'that I have as much to give as the other person – that I can do more than I ever believed.'

The older men who travel to Ireland and back as members of The Long Distance Gang learn that they can set out to plan something and do it, that life can be more than dreams and memories and getting drunk. They learn that they can become film-makers and presenters and can speak to university students and cinema audiences. These partners not only learn, but they remember and reclaim things about themselves. The men pick up bits of their lives long discarded as seemingly impossible, going out alone to catch a tram into town, visiting friends at home or in hospital, arranging a funeral, socialising at the Irish Centre.

Pat, Sean and others reflect on their achievements: 'I used to stay in my room all the time. Now I enjoy nothing more than getting into town and meeting up with a few old friends here and there.' They also begin to view their experience through a wider lens and to see that they are not the 'failures' society defines them as.

Workers learn the damage of labelling people, how this limits and lowers everyone. They come to see how, where professionals do residential work and take on the roles and use the language of institutional care, then they naturally end up assuming that all they do in their work is positive, until something comes along – The Long Distance Gang partnership – which operates 'outside of the givens' and in quite a different way.

And although threatening at first, perhaps, this alliance proves the golden opportunity that leads to a revisiting of those values supplied as part and parcel of the worker role – to a questioning of 'whose values and for whose benefit?' It seeds a process of growing and learning.

Nes and Julie learn to keep faith with their own experience, no matter how uncertain the 'experts' of their ideas! And they see further and rejoice in the knowledge that ordinary people hold the keys to their own solutions.

Trish's self-understanding helps hundreds of families in Nottinghamshire:

> ...partnership is valuable, especially when like-minded people work together for the same goals. I have learned about my own strength and determination – the more I speak to other people, the more the need for support and services is reinforced and this heightens my resolve even more. Coming into contact with other families means that a sense of community is formed where raw emotion is shared. The tidal wave of emotion that sweeps over me from other families adds to my own very deep emotions.

Trish learns about how passionate she is as a mother, and how this passion can be used for the benefit of other people as well as her own family:

> People who don't know Emma see a child with learning difficulties and challenging behaviour who looks different. When I and my family and those that know Emma look at her we see love, laughter and mischief – 'rainbows and glitter'.
>
> As the mother tiger, I have to know that my cub is in safe hands so I can get on with the challenging. As a parent I change from wanting to aggressively defend my child to wanting to understand other people's attitudes and how to change them. The initial response to having your child threatened in any way is to lash out to defend them. I learn that this potentially alienates people and I want to help them to understand so I learn to present what I feel in a different way and to temper this according to who I am talking to.

Trish learns about her own discernment:

> I have to understand how other people work and where they are coming from in order to get the best out of them – as well as other organisations assessing us. I become, without realising, an assessor of them. I begin to discern where people's values lie and how best to work with them and support them in their journey of understanding.
>
> ...expertise? You go into a partnership thinking that you know nothing and that professionals know everything and you realise that you do know a lot and that gives the confidence to move forward.

Stephen learns the value of reflection on his own life:

> You see the best of people in the worst of circumstances. It amazes me the resilience and tenacity of human beings and I am inspired by them.

It makes me appreciate and stop and think about my own situation. You can never truly prepare for these drastic changes in circumstances that people face.

Reshma and Sherma find the experience of working in partnership together to be very enriching. Reshma learns 'to be more challenging of situations that occur in partnerships.' Sherma recognises 'that working in partnership requires a high level of commitment, time, patience and collaborative problem-solving, each person has to be respected for the strengths they have and for the contributions they make to the end goal.' Reshma and Sherma reflect that:

> ...for any partnership to be successful it is important to have open and honest conversations with each other. From our experience we would strongly suggest that a high level of trust and honesty is needed to ensure that we work well together as partners.

June brings a very different perspective through her experience of situations that have been far from ideal and which have left her feeling disappointed and let down:

> I find it difficult, particularly where competing agendas can result in mistrust because situations are contrived. Take the increasing emphasis on alliances where service users and carers are required to meet together in supposed partnership working at the behest of the providers and commissioners. There is a danger of losing the specific issues for the different interest groups. Growing spaces need some 'separate spaces' too – a sort of 'me' time.

The experience of being in partnerships either encourages people to be open and trusting or it has the exact opposite effect and makes people want to retreat. This really does show the crucial importance of getting partnership working right.

Mark Lymbery reflects as an academic partner on his own learning through working in partnership with Advocacy In Action:

> I can also acknowledge my personal learning from working with service users. For example, I recognise that it has enabled me to present – and be accepted – as a more rounded human being to students. It has also enabled me to recognise my own human vulnerability and the centrality of this to my personality. If we seek to argue that the nature of social work is based on an interaction between human beings, this has to be

considered as a good thing! We are, after all, seeking to enable students to become warm and empathic human beings, capable of engaging productively with people experiencing intense difficulty and pain.

Advocacy In Action have learned much about power through their work with universities and other partners, what it feels like to hold power or to be in situations where power is withheld.

> Power is a difficult thing to talk about. It comes in various shapes, sizes, disguises. We have come to understand that bad power is difficult to deal with and takes ages to get rid of. Bad power leaves a big hole when it's pulled out. It can feel very scary. So we can usually tell when we are growing bad power in our spaces. Good power on the other hand is easy to grow, easy to spread around, and it just fills up again if you give it away. We learn to cultivate good power within one another. Advocacy In Action knows that the seeds of good and bad power are to be found in any person and any partnership. We just need to be able to identify and choose between all the different varieties.

In Sean's final months, it is the *power of living within dying* that brings learning to all partners.

Nes learns that his own experience is important and valuable to Sean and that he is counted as one of Sean's close friends: '...*am* I important – do people *really* want to listen to me?' Sean learns that he has value. He comes to grow through the mutual power of giving and receiving within friendships and relationships in a way he has cut himself off from for many years. He discovers too that the roots of family go much deeper than he has been willing to acknowledge. His final wishes encompass the daughter abandoned as a child. It is Gaynor who his arms wrap themselves around, from within the depths of his unconsciousness, as she makes it to his bedside for the last hours of his life. And although never put in to words, all his partners trust that Sean has died in a state of self-forgiveness, understanding perhaps it was not all 'his fault'.

We can say with confidence, however, that Sean surely knew his story would live on after him – through his film, through the seeds of memory quickening in others, and through the growing spaces and understandings he inhabits in this book. As Dave Milburn reflects, Sean's experiences in his final months enrich rather than deplete him and, ultimately, it is through his illness and his death that Sean visibly blossoms to become the person with power to move and inspire all around him, the person in charge of his own dying.

Julie finds out what a formidable fighter she can be when the quality of a friend's life and death depend on it. She also learns about the power of mortality and can place it where it belongs in her own life. Finally, Julie reclaims though Sean the power of unconditional love, and, where all boundaries are stripped away, the joy and friendship that blossom between the souls of kindred spirits.

Dave learns how deeply he is affected by the final months with Sean and other partners. Dave realises, through the writing up of these reflections, that he is filled to the brim with raw emotion and passion. He learns that, more than worker and manager, he is part of a family at '32', a belonging that defies any job description:

> ...on a personal note I will always hold the most vivid memory of staff and residents collectively gathering in the car park to move on to the cathedral and funeral mass. Incredibly smart, humble and united – so very rare – so very special – a real family. Do we realise it? In each of our own ways, very much so – yes.

In summary

Each of the partnerships and the individuals within them testify to the huge wealth that our own experience holds and how we have benefited from it.

Partners within a growing space cannot fail but to come to know themselves better, accepting this knowledge of self, protecting and nurturing it further.

LEARNING FROM AND ABOUT OTHERS

Advocacy In Action partners learn that:

> ...many people are surviving – just surviving – not all of them people like us. Some survivors wear professional hats. Some have power, and use it wisely or badly. We meet people in partnerships and have to choose whether to work with them or not. We learn that everyone is capable of being better – being who they want to be – if they get the chance to find this out. We also learn that you don't have to like people to work with them; it's about getting the job done.

But finding out about people often opens up some interest or quality that you can warm to. Good partnerships give us all the space to explore one another and grow common interests or aspirations. Partners don't have to befriend each other, only cultivate respect!

Advocacy In Action does recognise, however, that some people will never get there, and it is okay to let them go. They know not to get too cosy, not to pat partnerships on the back too often. But they can appreciate also a relevance and necessity of whole-hearted admiration. They find that they learn more about one another and about themselves in times of difficulty. They discover they can be together in uncomfortable spaces, with the right people.

'We recognise that everyone has got talents and we are open to be wholly amazed, to always see the possibility and the person.' When Julie meets Lee outside the Victoria Centre in 2003, her stunning use of space and backchat leave Julie mesmerised. Lee reckons that 'speaking to students' could be a better earner than begging! And so the partnership begins.

Advocacy In Action are humbled by the resilience and courage of ordinary people with extraordinary pressures.

> We put our backs against the wall and fight with them if they need them to. We think that we understand why people get angry, desperate and heartbroken in life and see how feeling positive and proud builds anyone up. We learn this – this anger, pride and power – from the challenges and achievements people have brought to us. And we feel such immense depth of understanding when others get close to us; even when they have dissimilar lives and lifestyles, we learn that you can be travelling the same journey but along different roads.

Practitioner partners tell Advocacy In Action:

> I will be the person who is prepared to believe in others and listen to what they have to and need to say.

> I will resolve to be the person who represents hope to the people I meet.

Sarah learns the value of individuals in partnership working: 'I have learned that partnership working can really make a difference to the individuals involved but also to others and organisations. Sadly the time needed to develop it is not always recognised by everyone involved.'

Ed learns to trust people and also to be forgiving: 'I've learned that people will do what they say they will – and if they don't – it may be because they have forgotten and are human like me – so it is okay for me to remind them!'

Long Distance Gang travellers also learn to trust on many levels and are able to move forward on the strength of that trust.

Nes learns deeply from the experience of making the film with his fellow travellers: 'the film exists as a space where stories are told and remembered, but maybe more importantly, as a reminder that, behind the rhetoric and polemic of battles taking place elsewhere, are the reality of people with lives and experiences.'

Nes comes away from the physical and creative journeys profoundly affected:

> I am consistently humbled during this process by the wit, bravery and intelligence of men who are largely invisible and forgotten both in land of settlement and in birth country – I hope some of this comes through the film.

Anil, Gina, Julie, Kevin, Nasira and Reshma reflect within PAct on what they observe that professional alliances and forums have taught them about one another and about partnership:

> The learning is to be mindful of the impact of words and actions, whether they represent your own personal values, or those of a group or an institution. Saying or doing things in the wrong way, even with the right spirit, can disempower *anyone*. However, we should know when we need to say the right things, whatever the cost!

PAct members continue:

> Workers are human too, some with equally distressed stories and backgrounds.
>
> Workers may be perceived as having power, but sometimes the system is bigger, therefore workers and professionals could also need a little help and moral support. Loss of power or identity can produce a shared experience of disempowerment for workers and service users. We should know this as common ground we all tread.
>
> We must also be aware of the power we hold in our various roles and that good power is there to be shared. And furthermore, when we share good power, we don't lose it – because it just doubles up in size

till it fills the room! Partnership gives us hope for the future and can help us see what a joy it is to work freely and well with others.

When practitioners engage with OPPS at presentations and at training events they take tremendous learning from their older partners:

> OPPS encourages me to push the power back and always give time to listen not impose my own ideas of what people need and want, to challenge the disregard for human dignity and to promote hope, promote dreams and promote respect. OPPS shows that older people can work together and work with us to make things better. I own that individual workers' perceptions can have overall impact on assessment, and I acknowledge the power in dictating what is beneficial for people we don't know – while negating their personal experience and self-expertise as unimportant.

> It is their life, not mine.

> I realise how we expect people to tell us very intimate and personal information without building up rapport or trust. Imagine me, the individual who finds it difficult to open up, now me the practitioner, trying to listen to other people's stories – when I myself cannot be open in the same way! Some people would rather not talk about their lives, any more than I want to talk about mine, but they are put into situations where they are obliged to. It is part of my job to ensure the process does not distance me from them. I acknowledge the importance of memories, and I remember when I leave someone that they will be left with their own memories of me. I commit to work in the trust that they will remember my involvement as being relevant, respectful, useful and positive.

Everyone in the OPPS partnership themselves learn from and about one another. Group supporter Reshma Patel reflects on how accomplishment in others adds to her own good feelings too. However, Reshma realises how relatively powerless service users are in the bigger scheme of things: '...comments from the interviews endorse that there will always be power differences when working with people who use services. The council must recognise and own this.'

Mary finds that:

> ...being involved has been for me personally a humbling experience. I have learned a lot in relation to user involvement and participation. I have seen that the involvement of older people, working with other older

people, makes such a difference to trust, confidence and empowerment. This has all given me huge job satisfaction. I feel really proud of how well the whole process and experience has worked and I believe that this is the only way forward.

OPPS have learned that professionals and older people can work together and that the voices of older people are received as powerful by professional audiences. They have learned that people of different ages and experiences can make a good team. They realise that professionals are people first and foremost, but people with occasionally conflicting roles. And finally OPPS learn with great joy that trust is rewarded when the powerful partners stick by what they say.

In his last months, Sean Travers Lynch wants others to learn from his life. He speaks to students at the local university. Student partners are deeply affected by him:

> Sean strikes me as a charmer, funny and witty! 'Corncrake Sean!' I find it hard not to cry. Julie's attitude is so liberating. I respect the shared commitment from all partners to fulfil Sean's last wishes. When I get home at night after hearing Sean's story, I weep. I will never forget Sean − a humble, noble and vibrant spirit − I have learned so much from him.

After Sean's death, residents, volunteers and staff reflect with Julie, Nes and Dave on their partnership over the last year: '…death is just a part of living − Sean has shown us that we can be in control if we want to and that we can, any of us, choose how we die and more than this we can choose how we live.' The partnership helps professionals and workers appreciate that:

> …we should recognise that although there is policy for this or guidance for that − there is a human being with thoughts, feelings and aspirations stuck somewhere in the middle of all the bureaucracy. We must beware, in following the 'company line', not to make run of the mill responses to extraordinary people in out-of-the-ordinary circumstances.
>
> …we must question our role in other people's lives, acknowledge and meet the need for a deeper understanding of their difficult and different experiences, rather than make sweeping generalisations. We must respect too the right to make unwise decisions. And we, as professionals, should support those decisions, not pull back because we disagree.

What does Sean realise from others at the end? Perhaps he finally recognises that he can put his trust in people and not be totally betrayed. And it is only a feeling, but we surmise that Sean might say he takes at the last from others and into his own dear heart the green shoots of acceptance, and the growing promise of loving himself.

June sums up the potential of partnership working for better or worse:

> Where there is a shared value base, sharing of power within the limitations and the Social Model underpins the alliance – it is brilliant. Where one or all of these ingredients do not exist it can be a recipe for disaster.

The Asperger's Consultation Group are able to learn positive things about each other: 'We learn to trust. We are able to see different people perspectives. We learn about age differences and life experiences.' One group member learns that other people with Asperger's are good to work with and get to know: 'I learn that I can have a positive experience with people with Asperger's.'

Jeanette echoes this sentiment from working with people in EMAPP. She learns 'that people always surprise me – and that I enjoy re-learning from them.'

Advocacy In Action teaches in universities over Europe. Travellers, rough sleepers, survivors of care homes and hospitals, people with 'conditions' and 'differences' work in partnership to help others learn. An 'outstanding contribution' to social work education is rewarded through their appointments as university lecturers, consultants and regulators.

Student and practitioner partners are Advocacy In Action's hope for the future. The partners ask them what they have learned from them:

> On this day I listen – really listen – but I need to keep this up, not slip back into my own blinkered viewpoint. I have to look long and hard at myself, I have been passive and unseeing, I am ashamed of past practice. I question at times my values – when I have chosen not to speak out – chosen to do nothing. But I now appreciate that whether a worker or a client, if you have support and are believed, it makes all the difference.

'As partners – *equally experienced* – allies and survivors, we ask of ourselves: "How hard can it be to be good to one another?"' This 'being good to one another' perhaps best describes Advocacy In Action's enduring hope within its partnerships with hundreds of other service-user and community groups, with countless students, practitioners and policy-makers. They will and do travel anywhere to help the people who need them.

In summary

From anchors of self-knowledge, we reach out and learn about others, with others and from others, herein recognising the mutuality of giving and taking that characterises true partnership and human engagement.

Partners in a growing space have the opportunity to grow and blossom within the rich soil of this mutual experience and wisdom they cultivate together. All of the partners within this book celebrate that they have learned so much from one another.

Let us here suffice with a simple, heartfelt and mutual 'Thank you!'

Chapter 5

PERENNIAL PESTS AND GROWING TIPS!

PERENNIAL PESTS

Our partnerships blossom profusely with passion, insight, achievement and hope. But collaborations less well tended spread disappointments and disillusionment. The enemies of good alliance need prompt attention. Here are the warning signs to watch out for:

- Blinkered vision and values.

- Bad power.

- Fear.

- Lack of faith in self, partners' partnership or work in hand.

- Blame culture.

- 'We've always done it this way!'

- When shall we bring in the…service users, those with a disability, the council, black and minority ethnic groups, etc.? (Are you sure you haven't already left it too late?)

- Incorporation and colonisation.

- Arrogance or patronising attitudes, from *any* partner — a real enemy!

- Defeatism — 'can't do' attitudes.

- Abusing the partnership or the partners for personal gain or self-advancement.

JULIE'S GROWING TIPS

* Hope.

* Humility.

* Courage.

* Clear vision.

* Unconditional regard.

* Challenging behaviour.

* Passion and energy.

* Creativity.

* Integrity.

* Joy.

JACKIE'S GROWING TIPS

* Understand each other as much as the reason for the partnership.

* Allow people to be themselves and play to their own strengths.

* If you are a professional, be just that, professional, but be human too and warm in how you relate to all others in your partnerships.

* Make your partners feel valued and your partnership an enjoyable and validating space to be in.

* Allow people to contribute in a way that they feel comfortable with and that makes bystanders feel that they want to contribute.

* Know yourself and be prepared to understand but not judge others.

* There is no room for arrogance, but if it surfaces, challenge it in a way that is kind and not in a way to put the person down.

* Be true to your values.

* Never lose your passion.

THE PARTNERS' GROWING TIPS

- Be prepared to learn from each other.

- Be flexible when something comes up that is important to someone.

- Have a sense of humour! Laugh together.

- Allow ourselves to say no as well as yes.

- Allow the process to develop naturally. Don't force things.

- Listen and learn; critically reflect and analyse. Read this book!

- Be willing to openly share your effective (and ineffective) strategies.

- Be prepared to learn and to give honestly of yourself.

- Give 100 per cent – the more you give, the better the outcome.

- There is always the next hill to climb, so never think you have learned everything; there is always much to learn.

- Don't be afraid to be honest about your mistakes and to learn from them.

- Have the courage to work out when a particular partnership won't work and to withdraw from it rather than be compromised.

- Don't lose your passion as this is the rocket fuel you need.

- Be kind to yourself – everyone gets fed up sometimes!

- Partnerships are like a tapestry of different colours and textures, so don't expect the same things from all your partnerships.

- Have patience to allow the relationship to develop into partnership.

- Understand the personal emotions that partnership working may invoke.

CONCLUDING THOUGHTS
SPACE TO GROW FURTHER

MAKING OUR OWN GROWING SPACE

Coming from our two very different positions to write a book together has been a positive challenge that has occasionally tested our personal relationship and prompted us to examine it at a much deeper level. This has felt uncomfortable at times, but has been ultimately enlightening and made our relationship healthier as a result.

Jackie writes

I have given a lot of thought while we have been writing this book to how I as a professional worker within both a professional social care and then an academic arena feel about working in partnerships. To be completely honest, they give me a lot of joy but also at times a lot of grief! I am the person who is regarded as having the power, but I often don't feel this myself. What I feel is that I have responsibility rather than power. I feel that I have often had to compromise to make things work. I do not have the luxury of a position where I can choose what to work on and who with, although I do in fact work with some truly wonderful people and on some fantastic projects.

I feel that my role has at times been that of trying to find a 'middle way' rather than necessarily what I think is best initially. I have had to account for what I do in a way that other partners don't. As the programme leader of the PQ programme, I do feel that it is a privileged position, but more so I feel the weight of getting the programme right so it meets the learning needs of social workers, meets the necessary regulatory requirements and the requirements of the university. When I sit in the Stakeholder Board meetings, it is that weight that I feel. I like working in partnership with others but I am also charged to do this. I have to answer to employing agencies and service users and carers in a way that they don't to me.

Does this mean that these partnerships aren't true partnerships?

I don't think so. I think that we try to make them true partnerships but that people have different stakes in them. For me, they have to work and I will do everything that I can think of to make sure they do. I cannot walk away as it is my job to ensure they are successful. I have been fortunate in that I have worked in my partnerships with people who are equally as committed as myself to getting the best results we can. That is what has made the partnerships possible for us.

This book contains lots of wisdom and I have learned much from it, but I am still learning. I think that people underestimate how difficult it can be to work in partnership as so much that calls itself by that name is just looking at the surface of relationships or outcomes. How to be a true partner and nurture that in others is the aspiration, and I hope this book goes some way to encouraging you to aspire to this too.

Julie writes

I have the privilege of being able to put my principles first and foremost. Everything else I am willing to lose. I suppose working for no pay might seem to some a powerless option, but the reality is that I feel powerful because I can say 'no' to partnership when I choose, and to whom I choose. I will always see things through where I find there is room for people to grow and I will invest all my energy and commitment to making things work. But when I know the ground is dodgy or the space not a kindly one, then I have no hesitation in moving on. I have refused work and handed work back rather than compromise where the value base is wrong or when I know my colleagues and I are being used.

GROWING SPACES FOR ALL?

For the more formal and regulated partnerships, true 'growing spaces' may not be achievable in entirety. Expectations and outcomes are often imposed from outside. However, this does not mean that the space itself must be restricted or sterile. In such partnerships, it is the *journey* towards achieving the ends that becomes crucially important. All partnerships can have their own 'growing space', even if it only blossoms in the way people work together and value one another. Our book has contained examples of where outcomes aren't necessarily wanted by everyone but nonetheless people have been truly respected and open along the way. There is always room to grow through working together, if we are open to and respectful of the experience.

OVER TO YOU

Every partnership is unique and full of potential. We have been inspired by the partnerships within these pages and hope that you have too. Celebrate your own partnerships and cultivate lots of lovely new growing spaces. Please take what is of use to you from our book and with a breath of kindness, blow the rest away.

INDEX